Quickreads Presents:
Open Your Own Nail Salon

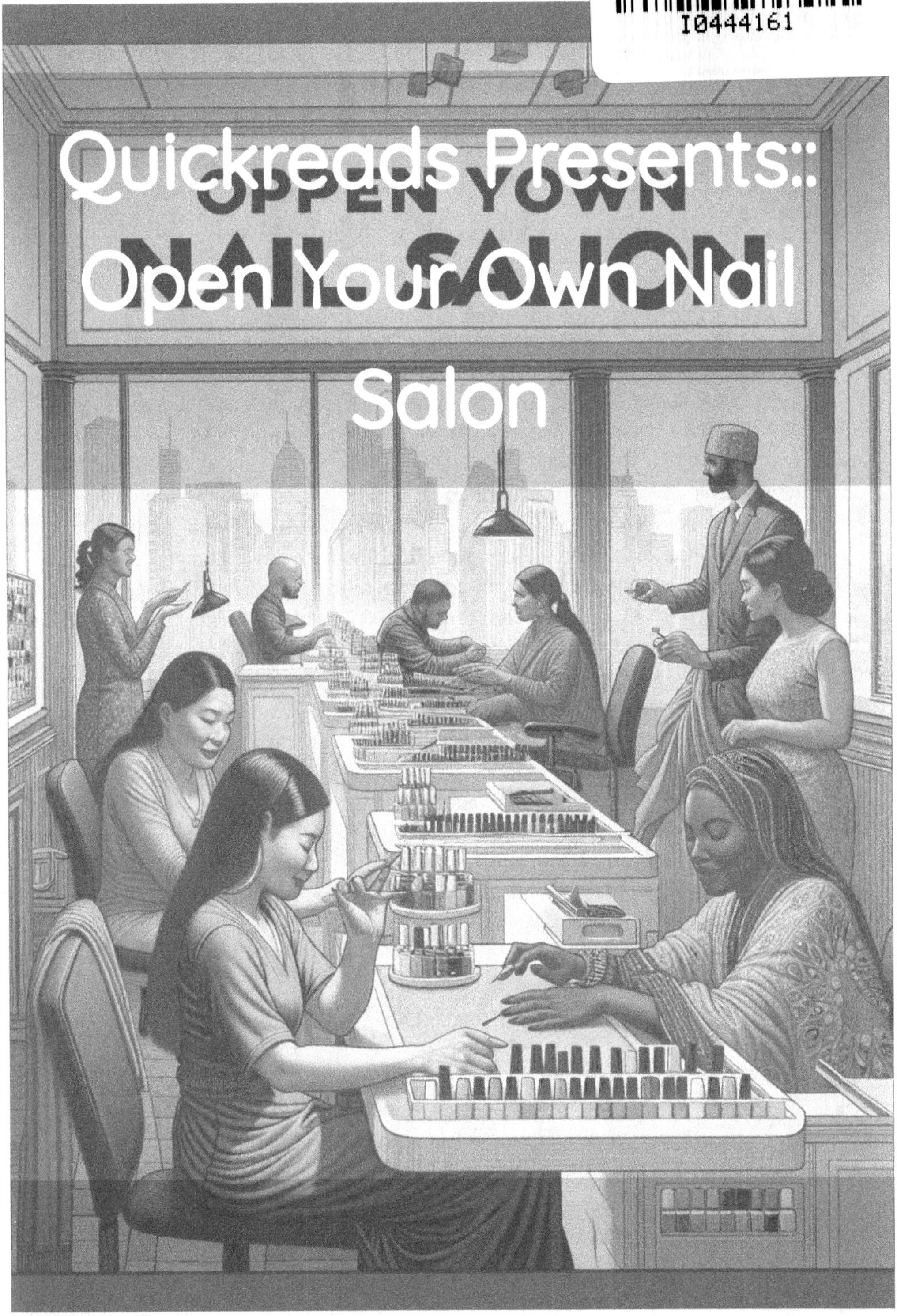

Quickreads Presents:: Open Your Own Nail Salon

Understanding the Nail Salon Industry

Historical Overview of Nail Salons

The historical evolution of nail salons can be traced back to ancient civilizations where nail care and embellishment were an integral part of grooming practices. Early evidence of nail care dates back to around 3000 BC in ancient Egypt, where high-ranking individuals adorned their nails with intricate designs using henna. Similarly, in ancient China during the Ming dynasty, nail polish made from beeswax, egg whites, gelatin, vegetable dyes, and flower petals was popular among the ruling class. Furthermore, nail adornment and care were also prevalent in ancient India, Persia, and other regions, signifying the cultural significance of nail aesthetics. The modern concept of nail salons began to take shape in the 19th century, particularly in France, where manicures became a symbol of status and sophistication. The French term 'manucure' gained prominence as specialized tools and techniques for nail shaping and decoration emerged. Fast forward to the 20th century, innovations in nail polish formulations and the introduction of artificial nails revolutionized the industry. The increasing popularity of manicures and pedicures during the mid-20th century led to the establishment of dedicated nail salons, catering to the growing demand for professional nail care services. In recent decades, the nail salon industry has experienced significant growth and diversification, with the incorporation of spa-like experiences, nail artistry, and the use of advanced technology in nail treatments. Understanding the historical trajectory of nail salons provides valuable insights into the cultural, social, and economic factors that have shaped the industry into what it is today.

Current Trends in Nail Care

In the nail salon industry, staying abreast of current trends in nail care is paramount for sustainable growth and continued relevance. As consumer preferences evolve, understanding and adapting to these trends can significantly impact a salon's success. One notable trend is the shift towards eco-friendly and non-toxic nail products. With increasing awareness of the potential health risks associated with certain chemicals found in traditional nail polishes and acrylics, consumers are seeking out salons that offer safer alternatives. This has led to a surge in demand for water-based, breathable, and vegan-friendly nail care options. Additionally, the incorporation of natural and organic ingredients in cuticle treatments and lotions has gained traction, appealing to environmentally conscious clientele. The rise of nail art as a form of self-expression has also influenced trends in nail care. Intricate designs, including hand-painted motifs, 3D embellishments, and sculptural elements, have become increasingly popular, providing opportunities for salons to showcase creativity and artistry. Moreover, the adoption of advanced technology in nail care processes has revolutionized the industry. Techniques such as gel manicures, dip powder applications, and digital nail printing have enabled salons to offer durable, customizable, and intricate designs, expanding the scope of nail services. Furthermore, there is an emerging emphasis on holistic nail care approaches that prioritize overall nail health and wellness. This includes the incorporation of treatments targeting nail strengthening, hydration, and restoration, aligning with the growing focus on self-care and well-being. Understanding and integrating these current trends into a salon's offerings can position it as a progressive and sought-after establishment within the competitive landscape of the nail care industry.

Regulatory Framework and Compliance Standards

The nail salon industry operates within a complex regulatory framework that governs various aspects of business operations to ensure compliance with health, safety, and labor standards. One of the primary regulations that nail salon owners must adhere to is related to sanitation and hygiene practices. This includes maintaining clean and sterilized tools, implementing proper handwashing protocols, and adhering to strict disinfection procedures for footbaths and workstations. Compliance with these regulations is imperative to prevent the spread of infections and diseases among customers and salon employees.

Additionally, nail salons are subject to labor laws and employment regulations that dictate fair wages, working hours, and occupational safety. It is vital for salon owners to stay abreast of labor standards to create a safe and equitable work environment while avoiding potential legal repercussions. Furthermore, licensing requirements for nail technicians vary by state and country, necessitating a thorough understanding of the qualifications and certifications needed to practice legally within the industry.

Environmental regulations also play a crucial role in the operation of nail salons, particularly concerning the use and disposal of chemicals. The proper handling and disposal of hazardous substances, such as acetone and other solvents, are essential to minimize environmental impact and protect public health.

To navigate this intricate web of regulations, salon owners must stay informed about local, state, and federal legislation pertaining to their area of operation. Establishing robust compliance protocols and documentation processes is key to ensuring adherence to standards and avoiding penalties or legal disputes. Moreover, ongoing training and education for staff on regulatory requirements can cultivate a culture of compliance within the workplace, promoting accountability and professionalism.

In conclusion, the regulatory framework and compliance standards governing the nail salon industry are multifaceted and demand meticulous attention to detail. By prioritizing regulatory compliance, salon owners can uphold the health and safety of their clientele and staff, foster a lawful and ethical work environment, and contribute to the overall integrity and reputation of the industry.

Market Analysis and Customer Segmentation

In examining the nail salon industry, it is vital to conduct a comprehensive market analysis alongside a thorough segmentation of the customer base. Market analysis involves researching current industry trends, consumer demands, competitor positioning, and economic forces that impact the nail salon sector. This necessitates a deep exploration of the demographic, geographic, and psychographic variables that characterize the diverse customer base of nail salons. Understanding the customer segments allows for targeted marketing strategies, personalized service offerings, and optimized resource allocation.

The market analysis begins by assessing the size and growth potential of the nail salon industry at both a local and national level. Factors such as population demographics, income levels, urbanization rates, and cultural influences are significant determinants of market demand. Furthermore, consideration must be given to consumer preferences, spending patterns, and lifestyle choices that impact the uptake of nail salon services.

Customer segmentation is a pivotal component of market analysis, as it involves categorizing consumers into distinct groups based on various characteristics. Geodemographic segmentation considers factors such as age, gender, income, occupation, and family size to define target customer clusters. Psychographic segmentation delves into the attitudes, values, personalities, and lifestyles of consumers, enabling the identification of psychological drivers that influence their grooming habits and preferences.

Segmenting customers also entails an understanding of behavioral patterns, such as frequency of salon visits, types of treatments sought, brand loyalty, and responsiveness to promotional efforts. By analyzing these dimensions, nail salon businesses can tailor their services, communication, and pricing to resonate with specific customer groups, fostering enhanced satisfaction and loyalty. Moreover, this segmentation facilitates the identification of high-value customer segments who yield the greatest profitability and long-term potential.

Conducting a meticulous market analysis and customer segmentation equips nail salon entrepreneurs with actionable insights to refine business strategies, allocate resources efficiently, and capitalize on untapped market niches. It enables the customization of services and experiences to cater to diverse customer needs while gaining a competitive edge in the dynamic landscape of the nail salon industry.

Technology and Innovation in Nail Salon Services

The nail salon industry has witnessed a transformative shift with the integration of advanced technologies and innovative practices aimed at enhancing the overall customer experience and operational efficiency. Technological advancements have revolutionized various aspects of nail salon services, ranging from the design and application of nail art to the management of appointments and inventory. This section delves into the multifaceted impact of technology on nail salon services, highlighting key innovations and their implications. Advanced digital imaging and printing technologies have redefined the landscape of nail art, allowing for intricate designs and personalized patterns to be created with remarkable precision. High-definition cameras and 3D scanning tools enable nail technicians to capture detailed images of clients' nail surfaces, facilitating the seamless recreation of desired designs. Furthermore, the introduction of automated nail polish applicators and nail art printers has significantly expedited the process of adorning nails, ensuring consistent quality and minimizing human error. Beyond ornamentation, technology has also revolutionized the health and safety aspects of nail services. Innovative ventilation systems and air purification technologies mitigate the exposure to hazardous fumes and chemicals, fostering a healthier environment for both clients and technicians. Moreover, the utilization of LED curing lamps has accelerated the drying process for gel manicures, reducing the wait time for patrons and optimizing workflow efficiency. The convergence of technology and data analytics has empowered nail salon businesses to streamline their operations and personalize customer experiences. Integrated management software and mobile applications have simplified appointment scheduling, inventory tracking, and customer relationship management. These platforms leverage big data analytics to discern consumer preferences, enabling targeted marketing campaigns and customized service recommendations. Additionally, the adoption of contactless payment systems and digital invoicing has enhanced transaction security and convenience, aligning with contemporary financial standards. Looking ahead, the potential synergy between virtual reality and augmented reality technologies offers exciting prospects for immersive nail art visualization and interactive client consultations. In conclusion, the integration of cutting-edge technologies and inventive practices is reshaping the nail salon landscape, enriching artistic possibilities, elevating service standards, and redefining operational norms.

Professional Associations and Industry Networks

Within the nail salon industry, professional associations and industry networks play a vital role in fostering collaboration, knowledge sharing, and skill development among practitioners and business owners. These organizations provide valuable resources, support, and advocacy for members, contributing to the overall growth and sustainability of the industry.

Professional associations such as the Nails Industry Association and the International Nail Technicians Association serve as platforms for networking and continuing education. They offer access to workshops, seminars, and conferences where professionals can stay updated on the latest techniques, trends, and regulations in the nail care sector. Additionally, these associations often collaborate with leading suppliers and manufacturers to facilitate member-exclusive discounts on products and equipment.

Furthermore, industry networks like the Professional Nail Technicians Forum and the Salon Owners Alliance provide forums for exchanging best practices, troubleshooting operational challenges, and discussing industry-specific opportunities. Through these networks, stakeholders can engage in dialogue regarding ethical standards, quality assurance, and customer experience enhancement.

Participation in these groups can also lead to collaborative partnerships and mentorship opportunities, creating a supportive ecosystem for newcomers and seasoned entrepreneurs alike. Moreover, professional associations and industry networks often advocate for the industry on legislative and regulatory matters, representing the collective interests of their members and promoting equitable policies that benefit the entire nail salon community.

In summary, active engagement with professional associations and industry networks is crucial for staying abreast of industry advancements, fostering meaningful connections, and advocating for the sustainable growth of nail salons. By joining forces with like-minded peers and accessing the wealth of resources offered, salon owners and nail technicians can elevate their practices, contribute to industry innovation, and ultimately enhance the overall competitive landscape.

Environmental Sustainability Practices

The nail salon industry has witnessed a growing emphasis on environmental sustainability practices in recent years, driven by increasing awareness of the environmental impact of salon operations and the demand for eco-friendly alternatives from conscientious consumers. Environmental sustainability practices encompass a wide array of initiatives aimed at reducing the ecological footprint of nail salons. This includes the use of non-toxic and low-odor products, energy-efficient equipment, and waste reduction measures. Nail salon operators are increasingly recognizing the importance of adopting environmentally responsible practices to minimize their environmental impact and attract environmentally conscious clientele. The adoption of sustainable, biodegradable, and non-toxic products not only reduces exposure to harmful chemicals for both salon workers and customers but also demonstrates a commitment to environmental stewardship. Additionally, implementing energy-saving measures such as LED lighting, efficient HVAC systems, and water-conserving fixtures can contribute to significant cost savings while reducing the salon's overall energy consumption. Furthermore, waste reduction and recycling programs can be implemented to manage and lessen the environmental impact of materials such as packaging, paper, and plastics. Some salons have also embraced initiatives like composting organic waste and utilizing eco-friendly cleaning products to further enhance their sustainability efforts. Collaborating with suppliers that adhere to environmentally responsible practices and sourcing products with minimal packaging are integral components of an environmentally sustainable supply chain in the nail salon industry. By proactively pursuing these measures, nail salon businesses can align with the growing global movement towards sustainability and distinguish themselves as responsible corporate citizens in the eyes of environmentally conscious consumers. Embracing environmental sustainability practices not only contributes to the health and well-being of individuals within the salon environment but also demonstrates a commitment to fostering a healthier planet for future generations.

Supply Chain Management in Nail Salon Industry

Supply chain management in the nail salon industry is a critical aspect that influences the procurement, distribution, and management of all products and resources essential for providing nail care services. The efficient management of the supply chain ensures that the salon has access to high-quality products, tools, and equipment while maintaining cost-effectiveness and sustainability. This section explores the intricate details of supply chain management within the nail salon industry, delving into the key components that contribute to operational success.

Procurement plays a pivotal role in supply chain management, encompassing the sourcing, purchasing, and selection of products such as nail polishes, gels, lotions, and other consumables. Establishing strong relationships with reputable suppliers and wholesalers is paramount to ensure a constant supply of top-grade materials that meet safety and quality standards. Moreover, strategic sourcing practices can lead to competitive pricing and favorable terms, ultimately impacting the salon's profitability.

Inventory management is another crucial element in the supply chain, as it directly influences the availability of products and tools essential for nail treatments. Implementing effective inventory control systems, such as RFID technology or barcode scanning, enables accurate tracking of stock levels and timely reordering to prevent stockouts. Proper inventory management also aids in minimizing wastage and optimizing space within the salon premises.

Distribution logistics are integral in ensuring that the salon receives deliveries in a timely manner and that products are efficiently utilized without excess holding costs. This involves coordinating with suppliers, managing transportation methods, and streamlining the delivery process to maintain a seamless flow of supplies. Adopting environmentally friendly packaging and shipment practices aligns with sustainable initiatives, contributing to the overall eco-friendly ethos of the salon.

In conclusion, supply chain management is an indispensable component of operating a successful nail salon, intertwining procurement, inventory management, and distribution logistics to uphold the availability of premium products while optimizing costs and supporting environmental sustainability efforts.

Revenue Models and Pricing Strategies

In the nail salon industry, revenue models and pricing strategies play a pivotal role in determining the financial success of the business. It is essential for salon owners to carefully consider various revenue models that align with their target market and differentiate their services from competitors. One common revenue model is the traditional fee-for-service approach, where customers pay for specific nail treatments such as manicures, pedicures, or nail art. Another approach gaining popularity is the subscription-based model, offering clients unlimited access to certain treatments for a monthly fee. This model fosters customer loyalty and provides a predictable stream of revenue. Furthermore, bundling services into packages or creating add-on services can be lucrative strategies to increase average transaction value.

Pricing strategies in the nail salon industry encompass a delicate balance between maintaining profitability and ensuring affordability for customers. Factors such as location, demographic profile of the clientele, cost of supplies, and competition influence pricing decisions. Utilizing tiered pricing based on the complexity of services or the level of expertise of technicians can optimize resource utilization and cater to varying customer needs. It's imperative to conduct thorough market analysis to set competitive prices while also considering the perceived value of services to justify premium pricing for specialized or luxury treatments. Moreover, implementing dynamic pricing techniques that adjust prices based on demand fluctuations or offering seasonal promotions and loyalty programs can stimulate sales and customer retention.

Integrated software systems can aid in analyzing sales data, customer preferences, and booking patterns to refine pricing strategies. Leveraging technology to implement online booking platforms and mobile applications not only enhances customer convenience but also facilitates upselling and personalized offerings. Additionally, exploring partnership opportunities with complementary businesses such as beauty salons, spas, or fashion retailers can broaden the revenue streams through cross-promotions and collaborative service packages. The synergy created by such alliances can attract new customer segments and diversify the revenue base.

As the nail salon industry continues to evolve, it becomes crucial for stakeholders to adapt and innovate revenue models and pricing strategies to remain competitive. By embracing trends such as environmentally sustainable practices and investing in training to offer specialized services, nail salons can position themselves as premium destinations, allowing them to command premium pricing and thereby increase revenue potential. Ultimately, a meticulously crafted revenue model supported by dynamic pricing strategies will fortify the financial viability and growth prospects of nail salon businesses.

Future Forecasts and Emerging Opportunities

The nail salon industry is poised for significant growth and evolution in the coming years. As society places increasing emphasis on self-care and grooming, the demand for professional nail services is expected to rise steadily. Additionally, the growing awareness of the importance of hygiene and sanitation will compel salons to invest in advanced sterilization technologies and practices, thereby ensuring the safety of their clients.

Moreover, the integration of technology into nail salon operations presents myriad opportunities for streamlining appointment bookings, inventory management, and customer relations. For instance, the adoption of booking platforms and mobile applications will enhance the convenience and accessibility of nail services, catering to the preferences of tech-savvy clientele.

Furthermore, the emergence of eco-friendly and non-toxic nail care products aligns with the shifting consumer mindset towards sustainability. Salons that prioritize environmentally conscious practices and offer organic, cruelty-free products are likely to attract a discerning customer base seeking ethical and health-conscious alternatives.

In terms of market expansion, the untapped potential in male grooming represents a promising avenue for diversification. With changing societal norms and an increasing number of men seeking grooming services, salons can capitalize on this demographic by offering specialized treatments and tailored experiences to cater to their unique needs.

Additionally, the globalization of beauty trends presents an opportunity for salons to incorporate diverse cultural influences and techniques into their service offerings, appealing to a broader client base and staying at the forefront of innovation.

As the industry continues to evolve, it is imperative for nail salon owners and operators to stay abreast of these forecasts and emerging opportunities, adapt to new demands, and proactively innovate in order to remain competitive and meet the evolving needs of their clientele.

Quickreads Presents:: Open Your Own Nail Salon

Developing a Business Plan

Market Analysis and Trends

The market analysis and trends section is a critical component of the nail salon business plan, providing an in-depth examination of the industry landscape. It involves evaluating the current state of the nail salon market, including market size, growth trends, and key drivers shaping its trajectory. This analysis delves into the demand for nail care services, consumer preferences, and emerging trends within the beauty and wellness sector. Leveraging statistical data, industry reports, and market surveys, this section aims to identify market opportunities and potential challenges. It also explores the impact of external factors such as economic conditions, technological advancements, and sociocultural shifts on the nail salon market. Furthermore, it entails forecasting future market trends and demands, enabling the business to adapt and innovate proactively.

In conducting a comprehensive market analysis, it is imperative to segment the target market based on demographics, psychographics, and consumer behavior. By understanding the distinct preferences and needs of different market segments, the nail salon can tailor its services and marketing strategies effectively. Additionally, utilizing tools such as SWOT (Strengths, Weaknesses, Opportunities, Threats) analysis and PESTLE (Political, Economic, Social, Technological, Legal, Environmental) framework facilitates a holistic assessment of the market environment. This section should also include a detailed examination of customer buying patterns, frequency of visits, and average spending per visit, providing valuable insights into revenue potential and customer loyalty.

Moreover, the market analysis delves into the competitive landscape, identifying existing and potential competitors within the local and broader market. Analyzing their strengths, weaknesses, and market positioning allows for a strategic comparison and differentiation of the nail salon's offerings. Additionally, a scrutiny of competitor pricing strategies, service portfolios, and customer engagement approaches assists in setting competitive pricing and developing unique selling propositions. Finally, by benchmarking against industry leaders and best practices, the market analysis aids in establishing benchmarks for performance and innovation, guiding the nail salon's ongoing development and growth strategy.

Competitor Analysis

Competitor analysis is a critical component of the strategic planning process for any nail salon business. This in-depth examination involves identifying and evaluating the strengths and weaknesses of current and potential competitors within the market. The purpose of this analysis is to gain a comprehensive understanding of the competitive landscape, assess the market positioning of key rivals, and ultimately identify opportunities to gain a competitive advantage.

To conduct an effective competitor analysis, it is essential to begin by identifying direct and indirect competitors. Direct competitors are those establishments that offer similar nail salon services and directly compete for the same target market. Indirect competitors may include businesses offering alternative services or products that could potentially divert consumer spending from nail salon services.

Once the relevant competitors have been identified, it is imperative to gather detailed information about their business operations, such as pricing strategies, service offerings, customer demographics, marketing initiatives, and brand positioning. This data can be obtained through a combination of market research, industry reports, and direct observation of competitors' establishments.

The next step in the analysis involves assessing the strengths and weaknesses of each competitor. Understanding the strengths of competitors can provide valuable insights into best practices, potential threats to the business, and areas for improvement. Conversely, identifying the weaknesses of competitors can uncover opportunities to differentiate the nail salon business by addressing unmet needs or enhancing existing services.

Furthermore, it is crucial to evaluate the market share and growth trends of key competitors. Analyzing market share provides clarity on the level of dominance exerted by competitors within specific segments of the market. In addition, monitoring growth trends allows for the prediction of potential shifts in consumer preferences and demand patterns.

Another vital aspect of competitor analysis is the assessment of their online presence and reputation. In today's digital age, a strong online presence can significantly impact consumer perceptions and decision-making. Evaluating competitors' websites, social media engagement, and online reviews can reveal key insights regarding their marketing strategies and customer satisfaction levels.

Ultimately, the findings from the competitor analysis serve as a foundation for shaping the nail salon's competitive strategy. By developing a deep understanding of the competitive landscape, the business can identify its unique selling propositions, refine its marketing messaging, adjust pricing strategies, and enhance overall service offerings to effectively position itself within the market. Moreover, ongoing competitor analysis is essential for maintaining a proactive approach to addressing evolving market dynamics and sustaining a competitive edge in the nail salon industry.

Target Market Identification

In the nail salon industry, understanding and identifying the target market is paramount for establishing a successful business. Target market identification involves thorough research and analysis to pinpoint the specific demographic, psychographic, and behavioral characteristics of the ideal customer base. Demographic factors such as age, gender, income level, and occupation play a crucial role in defining the target market. Understanding the psychographic attributes, including lifestyle choices, values, and preferences, provides deeper insights into consumer behavior and purchasing patterns. Furthermore, analyzing behavioral aspects such as loyalty to nail care services, frequency of salon visits, and spending habits enables a more comprehensive understanding of the target market. Leveraging geographic data can also aid in refining the target market by identifying location-specific preferences and demands. Engaging in market segmentation techniques allows for the categorization of potential customers into distinct groups based on shared characteristics, enabling tailored marketing strategies and service offerings.

Moreover, employing advanced analytics and market research tools assists in identifying niche markets with unmet needs and untapped potential. Utilizing customer surveys, focus groups, and observational studies aids in gathering valuable feedback and insights from the target market, unveiling unmet demands and emerging trends. This approach allows nail salon businesses to tailor their services, products, and marketing initiatives to satisfy the specific needs and desires of the identified target market, fostering customer loyalty and satisfaction.

Additionally, an in-depth understanding of the target market facilitates the development of compelling value propositions and unique selling points that resonate with the identified customer segment. By aligning the services, ambiance, and pricing structure with the preferences and expectations of the target market, nail salons can differentiate themselves from competitors and attract and retain loyal clientele.

Furthermore, staying abreast of evolving consumer trends, societal shifts, and cultural influences is imperative in continuously refining and adapting the target market identification process. Embracing technological advancements and digital platforms enables the collection of real-time data and consumer insights, empowering nail salon businesses to adapt swiftly to changing market dynamics and consumer preferences. Through proactive and adaptive target market identification strategies, nail salon entrepreneurs can position their businesses to thrive in a competitive landscape while delivering value and satisfaction to their discerning clientele.

Services and Pricing Structure

The services and pricing structure of a nail salon is a critical aspect that requires meticulous planning and strategic consideration. In this section, we will delve into the comprehensive framework for designing a diverse range of services and formulating an effective pricing strategy. It is imperative to conduct thorough market research to understand the demand for various nail care services within the target demographic. By analyzing industry trends and consumer preferences, salon owners can identify the most sought-after services and tailor their offerings to meet these needs. This may include manicures, pedicures, nail enhancements, nail art, and other specialized treatments such as gel or acrylic applications. Each service should be meticulously defined, outlining the specific procedures involved, the anticipated duration, and the materials used. A detailed pricing structure should then be established, factoring in the cost of labor, materials, overhead expenses, and desired profit margins. The pricing model should reflect the value proposition of the services offered, ensuring that it remains competitive within the local market while also justifying the quality and expertise provided by the salon. Additionally, considering bundling options or package deals can incentivize customers to opt for multiple services, thereby increasing revenue streams while fostering customer loyalty. Moreover, incorporating tiered pricing based on the level of complexity or specialization can effectively cater to diverse client preferences and budgets. It is essential to maintain flexibility in pricing strategies, allowing for periodic adjustments in response to evolving market dynamics and emerging trends. Furthermore, a transparent and easily comprehensible pricing menu should be presented to clients, outlining the different services offered along with their corresponding prices. This not only enhances transparency but also facilitates informed decision-making for customers. Highlighting any unique or signature services can further distinguish the salon from competitors, adding a distinctive appeal that resonates with the target market. Ultimately, a well-articulated services and pricing structure serves as a pivotal component in shaping the overall business positioning and generating sustainable revenue for the nail salon.

Operating Plan and Workflow

The operating plan and workflow of a nail salon are critical components that contribute to its overall success. This section focuses on the meticulous details involved in organizing and managing the day-to-day operations of the salon. The operating plan outlines the specific processes, procedures, and resources required to deliver exceptional nail care services to customers while ensuring efficient business operations.

Efficient workflow management is essential to optimize the productivity and effectiveness of the salon. It involves scheduling appointments, managing walk-in clients, and coordinating the work of nail technicians. The workflow encompasses customer intake, consultation, service delivery, and post-service follow-up. By implementing a well-defined workflow, the salon can ensure consistent service quality and customer satisfaction.

Furthermore, detailed attention should be given to staff training and development within the operating plan. This includes comprehensive training programs for nail technicians and front desk staff to ensure they are equipped with the necessary skills, knowledge, and customer service etiquette. Developing clear job descriptions, standard operating procedures, and performance evaluation methods will aid in maintaining a high level of professionalism and service excellence.

In addition, the operating plan should address inventory management, procurement of supplies, and maintenance of equipment and tools. Efficient supply chain management is crucial to avoid disruptions in service provision and maintain cost-effectiveness. This involves establishing relationships with reputable suppliers, monitoring inventory levels, and implementing inventory control measures to minimize wastage and ensure availability of essential products.

An integral aspect of the operating plan is the allocation of resources such as time, manpower, and physical space. Properly scheduling staff shifts, managing client appointments, and optimizing workspace layout contribute to smooth operations. Utilizing software systems for scheduling and resource allocation can enhance efficiency and minimize scheduling conflicts.

Implementing technology solutions for administrative tasks, client communication, and record-keeping is also a key consideration in the operating plan. This may involve utilizing point-of-sale systems, customer relationship management (CRM) software, and digital marketing platforms to streamline operations and improve customer engagement.

In conclusion, a well-crafted operating plan and workflow are vital for the successful functioning of a nail salon. It enables the salon to provide exceptional services, maintain operational efficiency, and ultimately achieve sustainable growth and profitability.

Risk Assessment and Management

In the nail salon industry, effective risk assessment and management are integral components of a comprehensive business plan. A meticulous analysis of potential risks allows salon owners to proactively identify, evaluate, and mitigate various threats that may impact the business operations. From occupational hazards related to chemical exposure and ergonomics to issues concerning client satisfaction and regulatory compliance, every aspect of the salon's activities must be carefully scrutinized to ensure a safe and sustainable environment. One key consideration involves conducting thorough assessments of potential financial, legal, operational, and reputational risks that the salon might face. This includes evaluating the costs associated with liability insurance, worker's compensation, and potential legal disputes, as well as assessing the impact of possible economic downturns or market fluctuations on the salon's revenue stream. Effective risk management involves implementing robust policies and protocols to minimize identified risks. This may include adhering to strict safety guidelines for handling and disposing of hazardous materials, maintaining proper ventilation systems, and providing ongoing staff training on safety procedures and protocol compliance. Additionally, establishing clear customer communication channels and feedback mechanisms is essential for addressing any dissatisfaction or concerns that could potentially harm the salon's reputation. By integrating risk mitigation strategies into the business plan, salon owners can foster a culture of accountability, transparency, and continuous improvement. Furthermore, regular reviews and updates of risk assessment processes should be conducted to keep abreast of changing industry standards, regulations, and emerging threats. Through proactive risk assessment and diligent management, salon owners can safeguard their business and enhance its long-term sustainability and success.

Technology Integration and Maintenance

In the ever-evolving landscape of the nail salon industry, technology has become an indispensable component for thriving businesses. From appointment scheduling and inventory management to customer relationship management and point-of-sale systems, technology integration plays a pivotal role in streamlining operations and enhancing the overall customer experience. Nail salons can leverage specialized salon management software that encompasses features such as appointment booking, employee scheduling, and client database management. Additionally, the integration of digital payment solutions not only expedites transactions but also minimizes errors and enhances financial transparency. Furthermore, the maintenance of technology infrastructure is paramount to ensure uninterrupted business operations. This entails regular hardware and software updates, data backups, and cybersecurity measures to safeguard sensitive customer information and prevent potential data breaches. Implementing robust maintenance protocols will mitigate downtime and safeguard against technological glitches that could adversely impact service delivery. Moreover, embracing emerging technologies such as mobile applications for appointment bookings and loyalty programs can further differentiate a nail salon in a competitive market, fostering customer engagement and loyalty. It is crucial for nail salon owners to stay abreast of technological advancements and evaluate their feasibility and potential impact on business efficacy. As technology continues to revolutionize the industry, strategic integration and meticulous maintenance are imperative to propel a nail salon towards sustained growth and success.

Regulatory Compliance Strategies

Compliance with regulatory standards and requirements is paramount in the nail salon industry. This section will delve into the intricate regulatory landscape that governs the operations of a nail salon and outline comprehensive strategies for ensuring full compliance. Nail salon owners must be well-versed in federal, state, and local regulations pertaining to sanitation, worker safety, chemical handling, and business licensing. It is imperative to maintain meticulous records and stay abreast of any legislative changes that may impact the business. Detailed employee training programs are crucial to ensure that staff members are knowledgeable about health and safety protocols, and that they adhere to all regulatory guidelines. Moreover, establishing strong relationships with regulatory agencies can be beneficial, as it allows for open communication and a proactive approach to compliance. Implementing regular internal audits and inspections can help identify and rectify any issues before they lead to potential violations. Additionally, investing in advanced software systems that track and monitor regulatory compliance can streamline the management process and provide valuable data for reporting and transparency. In a fast-evolving regulatory environment, staying vigilant and proactive is key to not only meeting current standards but also anticipating future regulatory changes and adapting swiftly. By prioritizing regulatory compliance strategies, nail salons can build a reputation for trustworthiness, integrity, and commitment to public health and safety.

Environmental Sustainability Initiatives

In today's business landscape, environmental sustainability is an increasingly vital aspect of any industry, and the nail salon sector is no exception. Implementing environmental sustainability initiatives in a nail salon business has numerous benefits, ranging from cost savings to improved public perception. This section will delve into various strategies for integrating environmental sustainability practices into the operation of a nail salon. Firstly, it is crucial to assess the environmental impact of the salon's activities, such as water usage, chemical disposal, and energy consumption. By conducting a comprehensive audit, salon owners can identify areas for improvement and implement targeted solutions. One key initiative is to switch to eco-friendly and non-toxic nail care products, thereby reducing the use of harmful chemicals that can negatively impact the environment. Additionally, implementing water-saving technologies and incorporating energy-efficient lighting and equipment can significantly reduce the salon's ecological footprint. Furthermore, adhering to proper waste management practices by recycling and properly disposing of hazardous materials demonstrates a commitment to environmental responsibility. Another essential aspect of environmental sustainability in a nail salon is educating and involving staff and clients in sustainable practices. Training employees on the importance of environmental conservation and providing them with the knowledge and tools to integrate sustainable methods into their work can lead to a more environmentally conscientious workforce. Encouraging clients to opt for eco-friendly services and products through educational materials and promotions can also contribute to the salon's sustainability efforts. Moreover, engaging in community outreach and partnerships with environmentally focused organizations can elevate the salon's standing as a leader in environmental sustainability within the local area. By spearheading or participating in eco-friendly initiatives, such as tree planting drives or fundraising for environmental causes, the salon can strengthen its ties to the community while championing sustainability. Embracing environmental sustainability in a nail salon business is not only socially responsible but also economically advantageous, as it can attract environmentally conscious clientele and enhance the overall reputation of the salon. Thus, by adopting and promoting environmental sustainability initiatives, nail salon owners can foster a more sustainable and enduring business model while contributing to the preservation of our planet.

Future Expansion and Growth Planning

In the dynamic and competitive nail salon industry, future expansion and growth planning are crucial for long-term success. This section will delve into strategic considerations and best practices for effectively scaling a nail salon business. To begin, it is imperative to conduct a comprehensive market analysis to identify potential opportunities for expansion. This should encompass studying demographic shifts, consumer preferences, and emerging trends within the industry.

Once potential growth areas have been identified, the development of a clear expansion strategy becomes paramount. This involves outlining specific goals, whether it be expanding into new geographical locations, introducing additional services, or diversifying the client base. Additionally, meticulous attention should be given to financial projections and budgeting to ensure that the expansion plans are financially viable.

As part of growth planning, it is essential to evaluate staffing requirements and operational capacity. This includes assessing the need for hiring and training additional personnel, as well as upgrading infrastructure and equipment to accommodate increased demand. Technological advancements should also be considered to streamline operations and enhance customer experience.

Furthermore, leveraging marketing and branding strategies becomes instrumental in promoting the expansion efforts. Creating a cohesive marketing plan tailored to the new target markets and implementing strategic promotional campaigns can facilitate the successful penetration of new territories.

Risk management and regulatory compliance remain critical components of expansion and growth planning. It is vital to assess potential risks associated with expansion, such as increased competition, economic fluctuations, and operational challenges, and develop contingency plans to mitigate these risks. Simultaneously, ensuring adherence to local regulations and obtaining necessary permits for expansion should be prioritized.

Lastly, maintaining a strong focus on sustainability and environmental responsibility during expansion is indispensable. Implementing environmentally conscious practices and embracing eco-friendly initiatives not only aligns with contemporary consumer expectations but also contributes to the long-term viability of the business.

By meticulously addressing the aforementioned considerations and proactively strategizing for future expansion, nail salon businesses can position themselves for sustained growth and relevance in the ever-evolving market landscape.

Quickreads Presents:: Open Your Own Nail Salon

Securing Financing and Loans

Assessing Financial Needs

Assessing the financial needs of a nail salon business is a critical step in securing the necessary funds for its establishment and growth. This assessment involves a comprehensive analysis of the costs associated with starting and operating the salon. Firstly, it requires a detailed breakdown of one-time startup expenses, such as leasing a space, purchasing equipment and supplies, hiring staff, obtaining licenses and permits, and setting up essential utilities. Additionally, ongoing operational costs, including rent, utilities, payroll, inventory, marketing, and insurance, must be factored into the evaluation. Secondly, projecting future expenses and cash flow is essential to determine the amount of funding required to sustain the business through the initial months or years until it becomes profitable. This projection entails forecasting revenues, monitoring industry trends, and anticipating potential economic challenges. Moreover, the assessment should consider unforeseen contingencies by incorporating a buffer for unexpected expenses or fluctuations in revenue. Furthermore, analyzing the capital needed for expansion, renovation, or diversification plans is crucial for long-term sustainability. Engaging in detailed market research to understand the average expenditures and profit margins within the nail salon industry is instrumental in deriving accurate estimations of financial requirements. Additionally, leveraging financial modeling techniques and software can aid in creating robust projections and in identifying potential areas of financial strain. Overall, a meticulous assessment of financial needs serves as the foundation for identifying the optimal loan options and developing a sound financial strategy for the successful establishment and operation of a nail salon.

Exploring Loan Options

When seeking capital to establish or expand a nail salon business, entrepreneurs must carefully explore a range of loan options to identify the most suitable financing solutions. Understanding the diverse landscape of financial products available is crucial in aligning the business's needs with the appropriate funding source. Firstly, traditional term loans from banks or credit unions offer fixed amounts of capital that are repaid over a specified period with interest. These loans are well-suited for long-term investments in large-scale equipment and facility expansion. Secondly, lines of credit provide flexible access to funds, allowing for quick and convenient borrowing as needed. Nail salon owners may find this option beneficial for managing fluctuations in working capital. Additionally, Small Business Administration (SBA) loans can be advantageous, as they offer favorable terms and reduced risk for lenders due to government backing. Importantly, entrepreneurs should also consider equipment financing, which specifically caters to the nail salon industry's need for specialized tools and machinery. By delving into the specifics of each loan type, business owners can identify the most advantageous option that addresses their unique requirements, financial standing, and future growth strategies.

Understanding Interest Rates and Terms

In the nail salon industry, understanding interest rates and terms is crucial when securing financing and loans for business operations. Interest rates represent the cost of borrowing money over time, expressed as a percentage of the principal loan amount. Entrepreneurs must comprehend the nuances of interest rates, including fixed versus variable rates, annual percentage rates (APR), and compounding frequencies. They should also be familiar with the impact of credit scores on interest rates, as individuals with higher credit scores typically receive more favorable lending terms. Furthermore, being informed about the current market interest rates enables entrepreneurs to negotiate with lenders effectively.

Term refers to the period over which a loan will be repaid, including the frequency of payments and the total duration. It is crucial for entrepreneurs to assess the implications of short-term versus long-term loans, understanding how the length of the term affects the total interest paid and monthly cash flow. Additionally, comprehending the structure of loan terms, such as amortization schedules and prepayment penalties, allows entrepreneurs to make informed decisions that align with their financial goals.

Moreover, entrepreneurs should evaluate the different types of interest rates available, including simple interest, compound interest, and fluctuating interest rates linked to market indexes. Understanding these variations empowers entrepreneurs to choose loan products that align with their risk tolerance and anticipated cash flows. In addition, entrepreneurs must delve into the details of collateralized versus unsecured loans, recognizing how the presence of collateral impacts both interest rates and loan approval likelihood.

Lastly, staying abreast of regulatory changes and economic indicators that influence interest rates is paramount in making proactive financial decisions. By being cognizant of government policies, inflation dynamics, and central bank actions, entrepreneurs can adapt their financing strategies to mitigate the impact of interest rate fluctuations on their business operations. Overall, a comprehensive understanding of interest rates and terms equips entrepreneurs with the knowledge needed to make sound financial decisions and optimize their business's financial health.

Preparing Loan Application Documentation

In the process of securing financing and loans for your nail salon business, a critical aspect revolves around effectively preparing the loan application documentation. This is where attention to detail, precision, and showcasing the financial health of your business comes into play. The documentation serves as a comprehensive snapshot of your business's financial position and future projections, which lenders will scrutinize carefully. At its core, the loan application package should include essential documents such as business financial statements, tax returns, cash flow projections, personal financial information from business owners, and a detailed business plan. These documents collectively provide an overview of the financial stability, creditworthiness, and growth potential of the nail salon. Ensuring that all documentation is accurate, complete, and well-organized is paramount. Lenders often require a business plan that outlines the vision, operational strategy, marketing approach, and financial forecasts of the nail salon. This plan should illustrate in-depth knowledge of the industry, market analysis, competitive landscape, and potential growth opportunities. Additionally, presenting clear and attainable financial projections, backed by thorough market research, can bolster the loan application. Financial statements, including balance sheets, income statements, and cash flow statements, should reflect the business's profitability, liquidity, and solvency. Accurate and up-to-date tax returns are imperative, demonstrating compliance with tax obligations and providing insight into the historical financial performance of the business. Moreover, disclosing personal financial information of business owners, such as personal tax returns, credit reports, and asset documentation, is standard practice, as it helps lenders evaluate the individuals' financial stability and commitments. Overall, meticulous attention to detail and accuracy in preparing the loan application documentation is pivotal in ensuring a favorable impression on potential lenders. Thoroughly review all documentation to eliminate errors or inconsistencies, as these could raise concerns among lenders. A well-prepared loan application package not only instills confidence in lenders but also demonstrates the seriousness and commitment of the business owners. In summary, the process of preparing loan application documentation demands discipline, transparency, and professionalism, contributing significantly to the successful acquisition of financing for your nail salon business.

Evaluating Collateral Requirements

In the process of securing financing for your nail salon business, it is essential to thoroughly evaluate the collateral requirements set forth by potential lenders. Collateral serves as a form of security for lenders, providing assurance that the loan will be repaid. As such, understanding and meeting collateral requirements is crucial to obtaining the necessary funding. The evaluation of collateral requirements involves a meticulous assessment of the assets that can be offered as security. This may include real estate, equipment, inventory, or accounts receivable. Each lender may have specific preferences regarding acceptable forms of collateral, and it is imperative to align your assets with their requirements.

Furthermore, the valuation of collateral plays a significant role in determining the loan amount and interest rates. Lenders typically conduct appraisals or assessments to ascertain the value of the proposed collateral. It is imperative for entrepreneurs to present accurate and updated valuations to strengthen their loan applications. Moreover, some lenders may impose certain restrictions on the types of collateral they accept, emphasizing the importance of aligning with their guidelines.

Additionally, entrepreneurs should consider the implications of offering personal assets as collateral. While this may enhance the credibility of the loan application, it also poses personal risk in the event of default. Understanding the ramifications of pledging personal assets is fundamental in assessing the overall feasibility of the financing arrangement. Furthermore, entrepreneurs must meticulously review the terms related to collateral, including any clauses that enable lenders to seize the pledged assets in the event of payment delinquency.

In conclusion, evaluating collateral requirements demands a comprehensive understanding of the assets available for security, as well as alignment with lender preferences. Entrepreneurs must focus on presenting accurate valuations, adhering to lender guidelines, and carefully considering the implications of pledging personal assets. By effectively evaluating collateral requirements, entrepreneurs can position themselves favorably in the loan application process and secure the necessary financing for their nail salon venture.

Comparing Loan Offers

When comparing loan offers for your nail salon business, it is crucial to conduct a comprehensive analysis of the terms and conditions presented by different lenders. The goal is to select a loan that aligns with the financial needs and growth objectives of your venture while minimizing the overall cost of borrowing. Begin by gathering loan proposals from multiple financial institutions, including banks, credit unions, and alternative lenders. Thoroughly review each offer, paying close attention to key factors such as interest rates, repayment terms, fees, and any specific requirements related to the nail salon industry. It's essential to evaluate the APR (Annual Percentage Rate) to accurately compare the total cost of each loan, factoring in both the interest rate and origination fees. Additionally, consider the potential impact of variable interest rates on your loan repayment and cash flow. Beyond the financial terms, assess the flexibility offered by each loan, including options for early repayment, refinancing, and potential penalties for late payments or defaults. Take the time to calculate the total amount repayable under each loan offer, considering the impact of compounding interest and any additional costs. Furthermore, recognize the importance of maintaining a positive credit profile and how your borrowing decisions may affect your business credit score. To facilitate an informed decision-making process, create a detailed comparison spreadsheet that outlines the various components of each loan offer. This will enable you to visualize the differences and similarities, making it easier to identify the most favorable option for your nail salon business. Consider seeking advice from financial experts or consultants who can assist in interpreting and comparing the intricacies of the loan offers. By conducting a thorough assessment and comparison of loan offers, you can effectively secure financing that positions your nail salon business for sustainable growth and success.

Negotiating with Lenders

Negotiating with lenders is a critical stage in the process of securing financing and loans for your nail salon business. This phase requires meticulous attention to detail and strategic communication to ensure favorable terms and conditions. As you engage in negotiations, it is essential to demonstrate your understanding of the loan offers and express a clear rationale for your counterproposals. Begin by conducting comprehensive research on current market rates, lending practices, and the specific terms offered by various financial institutions. Armed with this knowledge, you can confidently present your case and negotiate from a position of strength. Maintain a professional demeanor and articulate your requests with clarity, emphasizing the value your nail salon business brings to the community and the potential for long-term success. It is crucial to be prepared to discuss not only interest rates and repayment schedules but also any additional fees, prepayment penalties, and flexibility in case of unforeseen circumstances. Consider proposing personalized terms that align with your business's cash flow projections and revenue generation potential while minimizing risks. Throughout the negotiation process, make note of any adjustments to the initial loan offers and carefully scrutinize the revised terms to ensure they align with the agreed-upon parameters. Be proactive in seeking clarification on any ambiguous clauses and seek legal counsel if necessary to safeguard your interests. Make certain that the final loan agreement reflects the mutually beneficial terms negotiated. Remember that successful negotiation is founded on mutual respect and understanding; building a positive relationship with your lender sets the stage for future collaborations and continued financial support.

Reviewing Loan Agreements

When reviewing loan agreements in the context of securing financing for a nail salon business, meticulous attention to detail is paramount. The loan agreement serves as the legal documentation outlining the terms and conditions imposed by the lender upon the borrower. Understanding each clause, provision, and stipulation within the agreement is crucial to ensure full comprehension of the financial commitment being undertaken. Scrutinizing the loan agreement involves conducting a comprehensive analysis of various components. Firstly, the interest rate must be thoroughly examined, including whether it is fixed or variable, and the potential impact on repayment amounts over time. Additionally, understanding any associated fees, such as origination fees or prepayment penalties, is essential to avoid unexpected financial burdens. Moreover, the repayment schedule, including frequency and duration, should be carefully reviewed to align with the business's cash flow projections. Another critical aspect is the default terms, specifying the rights and remedies available to the lender in case of payment default. Evaluating collateral requirements, if applicable, ensures clarity regarding assets at risk in case of non-payment. Furthermore, covenants and restrictions delineated in the agreement demand close attention to comprehend any operational or financial limitations imposed on the business. It is imperative to seek professional legal or financial advice to clarify any ambiguous or complex clauses before signing the agreement. A diligent review of the loan agreement empowers the prospective borrower with knowledge and understanding, facilitating informed decision-making and mitigating potential future disputes or difficulties.

Finalizing Loan Acquisition

After thoroughly reviewing the loan agreements and ensuring alignment with the salon's financial goals and capabilities, the next critical step is finalizing the loan acquisition process. This phase requires meticulous attention to detail and adherence to legal and financial regulations. Once the loan terms have been negotiated and agreed upon, both parties will proceed with finalizing the documentation required for disbursement of funds.

The process of finalizing loan acquisition typically begins with the completion of the formal application documents. These may include promissory notes, security agreements, personal guarantees, and other legal instruments that formalize the obligations of both the borrower and the lender. During this stage, it is crucial to ensure accuracy and completeness in all documentation to facilitate a smooth and efficient transition to the funding phase.

Simultaneously, the loan provider will conduct a comprehensive review of the collateral offered by the salon to secure the loan. This step involves appraisals, inspections, and assessments to determine the value and condition of the collateral. The salon owner must be prepared to address any requirements or conditions set forth by the lender regarding the pledged assets.

Upon satisfaction of all documentation and collateral requirements, the finalization process progresses to the disbursement of funds. Lenders will typically outline the specific procedures for fund transfer, and it is essential for the salon owner to be well-informed about the expected timeline and method of disbursement. Clear communication and coordination between the salon's financial team and the lending institution are imperative to ensure seamless fund transfer.

Once the funds have been disbursed, meticulous record-keeping and financial management become paramount. The salon must establish designated accounts to manage the loan proceeds and adhere to any stipulations regarding fund utilization as specified in the loan agreement. Proactive budgeting and financial planning will aid in effectively managing the acquired funds and meeting the envisioned business objectives.

As the loan acquisition process culminates, the salon's financial team should maintain regular communication with the lender to address any queries or concerns. Additionally, consistent monitoring of the loan's performance and adherence to repayment schedules is vital to mitigate risks and uphold a positive rapport with the lender. Effective management of the borrowed funds serves as a testament to the salon's financial prudence and stability, laying a strong foundation for future financial endeavors.

Managing Debt Responsibly

Managing debt responsibly is a critical aspect of maintaining financial stability and ensuring the long-term success of your nail salon business. Once you have secured financing and acquired necessary loans, it is imperative to establish effective strategies for handling debt in a prudent manner. This section will delve into the key principles and best practices for managing debt responsibly in the context of a nail salon business.

One fundamental principle of managing debt responsibly is to prioritize the repayment of high-interest debts. By focusing on clearing debts with higher interest rates, you can minimize the overall cost of borrowing and allocate more resources towards growing your business. Additionally, creating a detailed debt repayment plan that outlines specific timelines and targets for each loan can help you stay organized and focused on reducing outstanding balances.

Another crucial strategy for responsible debt management is to maintain open communication with lenders. Establishing a transparent relationship with your creditors can provide opportunities for renegotiating terms or seeking alternative repayment arrangements if faced with unforeseen challenges. Proactive engagement with lenders can also demonstrate your commitment to fulfilling financial obligations, which can positively impact your creditworthiness.

Furthermore, implementing effective cash flow management practices is essential for sustaining healthy debt levels. Monitoring revenue inflows and outflows, optimizing inventory turnover, and controlling operating expenses are all integral components of sound financial management. By maintaining a strong cash position, you can mitigate the reliance on additional borrowing and build a solid foundation for future growth.

In the context of a nail salon business, it is paramount to align debt management strategies with revenue generation efforts. Continuously evaluating the return on investment for various business expenditures, such as marketing campaigns or equipment upgrades, is essential for making informed decisions about leveraging debt for strategic purposes. Balancing prudent debt utilization with sustainable revenue streams is pivotal for achieving long-term financial resilience.

Moreover, staying abreast of industry trends and regulatory changes can influence debt management strategies. Adapting to evolving market conditions and regulatory requirements can help mitigate potential risks associated with debt and enable proactive adjustments to business operations. Furthermore, seeking professional financial guidance from advisors or consultants can offer valuable insights for optimizing debt management within the unique dynamics of the nail salon industry.

Ultimately, exercising discipline and diligence in managing debt responsibly is indispensable for safeguarding the financial health and viability of your nail salon business. By adhering to prudent debt management principles, actively monitoring financial performance, and adapting to shifting economic landscapes, you can position your business for sustained growth and resilience in the competitive market.

Quickreads Presents:: Open Your Own Nail Salon

Selecting the Best Banks and Credit Unions for Funding

Identifying Financial Institutions

In identifying financial institutions for obtaining funding, it is crucial to conduct a comprehensive analysis of the available options. This process involves researching and evaluating banks and credit unions to determine their suitability for providing the necessary capital to support the nail salon business venture. Various factors must be considered, including the institution's reputation, financial stability, and track record in serving small businesses within the beauty industry. Additionally, it is imperative to examine the types of lending products and services offered by each institution and assess whether they align with the specific financing needs of the nail salon business. This entails scrutinizing the range of loan and credit options available, such as term loans, lines of credit, SBA loans, and other tailored financial solutions designed to meet the unique requirements of entrepreneurs in the beauty sector. Furthermore, the identification process should involve understanding the eligibility criteria and application processes associated with each financial institution. It is essential to discern the documentation requirements, credit score expectations, collateral specifications, and any other pertinent details related to securing financing from these institutions. By meticulously identifying and evaluating financial institutions, entrepreneurs can effectively navigate the landscape of funding options and make informed decisions that align with the strategic objectives of their nail salon business.

Analyzing Loan and Credit Options

In the nail salon industry, the analysis of loan and credit options is fundamental to the establishment and growth of a successful business. When considering financial assistance, entrepreneurs must conduct a comprehensive evaluation of various loan products and credit options offered by different financial institutions. This process involves meticulous scrutiny of the terms, conditions, and features associated with each financial instrument. It also necessitates a thorough understanding of the implications these options carry for the long-term financial health of the enterprise.

Lenders provide an array of loan products tailored to the specific needs of small businesses, including term loans, lines of credit, equipment financing, and Small Business

Administration (SBA) loans. Each option comes with its unique set of terms, interest rates, collateral requirements, and repayment schedules. Entrepreneurs must carefully weigh these factors against their business strategies and cash flow projections to determine the most suitable choice.

Similarly, credit options such as business credit cards, merchant cash advances, and trade credit play a pivotal role in meeting short-term operational expenses and handling unforeseen cash flow gaps. These options often come with varying interest rates, fees, and credit limits, which demand a diligent assessment to align with the business's financial objectives.

Furthermore, the analysis of loan and credit options extends beyond the quantitative aspects; it also encompasses an examination of the qualitative elements, including the reputation and reliability of the lending institutions. Assessing the track record and credibility of potential lenders is crucial in ensuring a transparent and supportive financial relationship.

Moreover, entrepreneurs must leverage financial advisory services or consult with industry professionals to grasp the intricacies of loan and credit options and make informed decisions. This entails engaging in detailed discussions concerning the implications of different financing choices on the business's capital structure, risk profile, and overall financial stability.

Ultimately, a meticulous analysis of loan and credit options empowers entrepreneurs to secure the most advantageous financial resources for their nail salon ventures, contributing to sustainable growth, operational resilience, and long-term success.

Evaluating Interest Rates and Terms

When establishing a nail salon business, evaluating interest rates and terms is a critical aspect of financial planning. Interest rates determine the cost of borrowing funds, while loan terms outline the conditions under which the loan is to be repaid. A thorough understanding of these factors is essential for making informed decisions regarding financing.

Interest rates can greatly impact the overall repayment amount. Whether opting for a fixed or variable rate, it's crucial to comprehend the potential fluctuations in monthly payments and the long-term implications on the business's finances. Comparing interest rates across different financial institutions enables entrepreneurs to identify competitive offers that align with their budgetary constraints.

Moreover, comprehending loan terms is imperative for avoiding future financial pitfalls. From the duration of the loan to potential penalties for early repayment, each term holds significant weight in the overall financial strategy. Entrepreneurs must carefully assess the impact of loan terms on cash flow and ensure they correspond to the business's projected revenue stream.

Assessing the relationship between interest rates and terms provides insights into the feasibility of acquiring funding and repaying loans within set time frames. It also aids in developing contingency plans to mitigate potential challenges. Through meticulous evaluation and comparison of interest rates and terms, entrepreneurs can secure financing that complements their operational needs and contributes to the salon's long-term financial stability.

Comparing Banking Services

In the process of selecting the best banks and credit unions for funding a nail salon business, one crucial aspect is the comparison of banking services. This involves a comprehensive evaluation of the range and quality of services offered by various financial institutions. Comparing banking services encompasses an analysis of essential features such as account types, transactional capabilities, and additional financial products. Additionally, it involves an examination of technological offerings, customer support, and accessibility.

When comparing banking services, it is imperative to consider the diverse needs of a nail salon business. This includes determining the types of accounts offered by different banks and credit unions, such as business checking accounts, savings accounts, and merchant services. Understanding the transactional capabilities is also critical, as it pertains to the efficiency and convenience of processing payments, managing payroll, and handling daily financial operations. Furthermore, evaluating additional financial products, such as business loans, lines of credit, and equipment financing, can provide insights into a financial institution's commitment to supporting small businesses in the nail salon industry.

Moreover, technological offerings play a significant role in modern banking services. Assessing online and mobile banking platforms, as well as the availability of digital payment solutions, is essential in streamlining financial management processes for a nail salon business. Seamless integration with accounting software, intuitive user interfaces, and robust security features are key factors to consider when comparing the technological aspects of banking services.

Customer support is another pivotal dimension in the comparison of banking services. The responsiveness and expertise of banking representatives, the availability of dedicated business banking support, and the provision of tailored financial advice can greatly impact the overall banking experience for a nail salon business owner. Accessibility considerations encompass the geographical presence of branches and ATMs, as well as the ease of conducting transactions and accessing financial resources remotely.

In conclusion, comparing banking services involves an intricate assessment of account types, transactional capabilities, additional financial products, technological offerings, customer support, and accessibility. By diligently scrutinizing these aspects, a nail salon business can make informed decisions regarding the selection of a financial institution that aligns with its specific operational and financial requirements.

Assessing Customer Support

In the nail salon industry, assessing the customer support provided by financial institutions is an essential aspect of selecting the best banks and credit unions for funding. Customer support encompasses a range of services that directly impact the overall banking experience for salon owners seeking financial assistance. It involves evaluating the responsiveness, knowledge, and professionalism of the institution's customer service representatives. When assessing customer support, it is imperative to consider various factors that contribute to a positive banking relationship. Firstly, responsiveness plays a pivotal role in ensuring that urgent queries or issues are promptly addressed. A bank or credit union with efficient customer support can provide timely assistance in navigating loan applications, addressing financial concerns, and resolving any potential issues that may arise. Secondly, the knowledge and expertise of customer service representatives are critical. Salon owners should seek institutions where representatives possess a comprehensive understanding of the unique financial needs and challenges faced by businesses in the nail industry. They should be able to provide tailored advice and solutions that align with the specific requirements of nail salon business operations. Professionalism is another fundamental aspect of customer support assessment. Banking institutions that prioritize professionalism demonstrate respect, courtesy, and integrity in their interactions with salon owners. This contributes to a positive and reassuring banking experience, fostering trust and confidence in the financial partnership. Additionally, an evaluation of customer support should consider the availability of multiple communication channels, such as phone, email, and live chat, to accommodate diverse preferences and urgent inquiries. Furthermore, the accessibility of customer support during non-traditional business hours can be advantageous for salon owners managing busy schedules. As technology continues to advance, the integration of digital support platforms and self-service options should also be evaluated to determine the convenience and efficiency of obtaining assistance. Overall, thorough assessment of customer support empowers salon owners to select financial institutions that prioritize exemplary service, proactive problem-solving, and effective communication, creating a foundation for a productive and collaborative banking relationship.

Understanding Fee Structures

In the context of securing funding for a nail salon business, the understanding of fee structures is paramount. Fee structures refer to the various charges and costs associated with maintaining accounts, processing transactions, and accessing banking services. It is essential for nail salon entrepreneurs to meticulously comprehend the fee structures offered by different banks and credit unions, as these fees can significantly impact the overall financial health and operational efficiency of the business.

When evaluating fee structures, it is imperative to consider both explicit and implicit fees. Explicit fees are those that are clearly disclosed by the financial institution, such as monthly maintenance fees, overdraft fees, ATM fees, and transaction charges. Understanding the nature and magnitude of explicit fees is crucial in gauging the affordability and suitability of a particular banking service.

Moreover, implicit fees, which may not be overtly stated, also play a significant role in determining the cost of banking. These may include hidden charges, opportunity costs, and foregone interest earnings due to minimum balance requirements or account restrictions. Entrepreneurs should conduct a comprehensive analysis to identify and quantify implicit fees, enabling them to make informed decisions regarding their banking relationships.

Furthermore, a deep understanding of fee structures necessitates an exploration of the potential impacts on cash flow and profitability. Excessive or unforeseen fees can erode profits and disrupt cash management, posing substantial risks to the financial sustainability of a nail salon business. Thus, entrepreneurs should carefully assess fee structures in alignment with anticipated transaction volumes and average balances to predict the financial implications accurately.

Additionally, the comparison of fee structures across multiple institutions is essential for making optimal financing decisions. By conducting thorough market research and soliciting proposals from various banks and credit unions, entrepreneurs can gain insights into the competitive landscape and negotiate favorable terms. This process involves scrutinizing fee schedules, waivers, and bundling options to identify the most cost-effective and flexible banking arrangements.

It is important to note that proactive communication with banking representatives is crucial for obtaining clarity on fee structures and negotiating customized solutions. Entrepreneurs should seek to establish transparent and collaborative relationships with financial institutions to address any ambiguities or concerns related to fee assessments. Furthermore, leveraging technology and digital banking platforms can provide visibility into fee structures, streamline expense tracking, and facilitate proactive management of financial obligations.

Ultimately, a nuanced comprehension of fee structures empowers nail salon entrepreneurs to make informed financial choices that align with their business objectives. By exercising diligence in evaluating, comparing, and negotiating fee arrangements, entrepreneurs can optimize their banking relationships, mitigate financial risks, and bolster the financial resilience of their ventures.

Reviewing Online Banking Capabilities

In the modern business landscape, online banking capabilities play a pivotal role in the financial operations of any enterprise. When selecting the best bank or credit union for funding, a thorough assessment of online banking features is essential to ensure seamless and efficient monetary management. Online banking capabilities encompass a wide array of services, ranging from basic account monitoring and transaction history to more advanced functionalities such as fund transfers, bill payments, and remote check deposits.

In reviewing online banking capabilities, it is imperative to evaluate the user interface and experience offered by the financial institution. A user-friendly and intuitively designed online platform facilitates swift navigation and streamlined access to critical financial data, contributing to enhanced operational productivity.

Furthermore, the functionality of mobile banking applications must be scrutinized to ascertain the compatibility with various devices and operating systems. A robust mobile banking app enables entrepreneurs to manage their financial affairs on-the-go, offering convenience and flexibility in executing transactions and accessing vital account information.

Security protocols represent a paramount aspect of online banking capabilities. A comprehensive review of the encryption methods, multi-factor authentication mechanisms, and adherence to industry security standards is crucial in safeguarding sensitive financial data from unauthorized access and cyber threats. Financial institutions must demonstrate a commitment to maintaining the integrity and confidentiality of their clients' information through state-of-the-art security measures.

Additionally, the integration of value-added services within the online banking framework enhances the overall banking experience for entrepreneurs. Access to financial planning tools, budgeting assistance, and customized reporting functionalities can significantly augment the utility of online banking platforms, empowering business owners in making well-informed financial decisions.

Moreover, the efficiency and reliability of online customer support channels should not be overlooked. The availability of responsive customer service via live chat, email, or phone can alleviate concerns and provide prompt resolutions to any technical issues encountered during online banking activities.

Ultimately, a comprehensive evaluation of online banking capabilities encompasses the assessment of accessibility, functionality, security, and supportive services. By leveraging the full potential of sophisticated online banking features, entrepreneurs can propel their business forward with confident and proficient financial management.

Examining Security Measures

In the digital era, security measures are paramount when selecting a financial institution for funding. Nail salon entrepreneurs must meticulously scrutinize the security protocols implemented by banks and credit unions to safeguard their sensitive financial data and assets. Firstly, it's essential to delve into the encryption methods utilized by the financial institutions. Advanced encryption technology such as AES (Advanced Encryption Standard) with a minimum of 256-bit encryption should be a top priority. This robust encryption standard ensures that any data transmitted over the internet or stored on servers remains secure and indecipherable to unauthorized personnel. Furthermore, multi-factor authentication plays a pivotal role in fortifying security. Financial institutions employing multi-factor authentication require multiple forms of verification, such as passwords, security tokens, or biometric scans, heightening the barrier against potential breaches. Alongside this, stringent access controls are vital in mitigating risks. Implementing role-based access controls restricts individuals within the organization from gaining unauthorized access to sensitive financial information. Additionally, regular security audits and compliance assessments must be conducted by the financial institutions to ensure adherence to industry standards and regulations, thus fostering trust and reliability. Continuous monitoring for fraud detection and prevention mechanisms is another significant aspect to consider. This involves real-time monitoring systems that can identify and alert anomalies in transactions, providing proactive defense against fraudulent activities. It's imperative to assess the physical security measures put in place by the financial institutions. This includes evaluating the security of their data centers, disaster recovery plans, and redundancy protocols to ensure the availability of services even in unforeseen circumstances. Lastly, staying abreast of the latest cybersecurity trends and threats is crucial. Financial institutions that invest in ongoing staff training and adopt cutting-edge security technologies demonstrate a commitment to safeguarding their clients' assets and sensitive information.

Considering Accessibility and Convenience

When considering the accessibility and convenience of a financial institution for funding, it is essential to assess various factors that can impact the overall operational efficiency and productivity of a nail salon business. Accessibility encompasses physical proximity to the bank or credit union, the availability of ATMs, and branch locations in relation to the salon's daily operations and your personal convenience. Ideally, select a financial institution with branches or ATMs situated within close proximity to the nail salon to facilitate quick and convenient access to banking services. Additionally, inquire about the accessibility of online banking platforms and mobile applications offered by the financial institution, as these digital tools can streamline transactions and account management, providing added convenience for business owners. Furthermore, evaluate the operating hours of the financial institution, ensuring that they align with the operational needs of the salon. Consider selecting a bank or credit union that offers extended or flexible hours to accommodate your schedule. In terms of convenience, consider the ease of conducting various financial activities such as making deposits, accessing account information, and processing payments. Evaluate the availability of self-service options, such as deposit-taking ATMs and mobile check deposit features, which can provide added convenience by eliminating the need for in-branch visits. Assess the availability of other convenient banking services such as courier services for deposit pick-ups or specialized business banking centers that cater to the unique needs of salon businesses. By carefully considering the accessibility and convenience factors in the selection of a financial institution, you can enhance operational efficiency and facilitate seamless financial transactions, ultimately contributing to the overall success of your nail salon business.

Negotiating Funding Agreements

As a nail salon entrepreneur, negotiating funding agreements is a critical aspect of securing the necessary capital to establish and grow your business. This process involves detailed discussions with potential lenders or investors to reach mutually beneficial terms for the provision of financial resources. Negotiating funding agreements requires a strategic approach and a comprehensive understanding of the various components involved.

The negotiation process begins with a thorough assessment of the specific financial requirements of your nail salon business. This includes determining the amount of funding needed, the purpose of the funds, and the projected timeline for repayment. Once these aspects are clearly defined, you can initiate discussions with potential financiers.

Effective negotiation of funding agreements necessitates a strong understanding of the financial products available in the market. It is crucial to evaluate and compare the terms offered by different financial institutions, considering factors such as interest rates, collateral requirements, repayment schedules, and associated fees. Armed with this knowledge, you can enter negotiations well-prepared and confident, able to articulate your financial needs and concerns effectively.

During negotiations, it is important to advocate for terms that align with the long-term interests of your nail salon business. This may involve seeking competitive interest rates, flexible repayment options, and favorable collateral conditions. Additionally, entrepreneurs should carefully consider the impact of covenants or restrictions imposed by lenders as part of the funding agreement. Negotiating favorable terms in these areas can greatly influence the financial sustainability of the business.

Furthermore, successful negotiation of funding agreements often hinges on the ability to communicate a compelling business case to potential financiers. This entails presenting a comprehensive business plan, detailing the viability and growth potential of the nail salon enterprise. Emphasizing key performance indicators, competitive advantages, and market opportunities can instill confidence in financiers and enhance the prospects of securing favorable funding terms.

In conclusion, negotiating funding agreements demands a combination of financial acumen, strategic planning, and persuasive communication. By meticulously assessing financial requirements, understanding available financial products, advocating for favorable terms, and presenting a compelling business case, nail salon entrepreneurs can position themselves for successful negotiations and secure the funding needed to thrive in the competitive beauty industry.

Quickreads Presents:: Open Your Own Nail Salon

Sourcing Equipment and Furniture

Identifying Essential Equipment

In the nail salon industry, identifying essential equipment is crucial to setting up a functional and efficient business. Key equipment includes manicure and pedicure stations, nail drying stations, ventilation systems, sterilization units, and ergonomic chairs for technicians and clients. Each piece of equipment serves a specific purpose in delivering high-quality nail services while ensuring the safety and comfort of both customers and staff.

When considering manicure and pedicure stations, factors such as design, durability, ergonomic features, and compatibility with different nail treatments should be taken into account. Ventilation systems play a vital role in maintaining air quality within the salon, effectively removing chemical fumes and dust to create a healthy working environment. Sterilization units are essential for maintaining strict hygiene standards, preventing the spread of infections, and ensuring the safety of clients.

Furthermore, the selection of nail drying stations should prioritize efficiency and client comfort, offering quick yet gentle drying processes to enhance the overall customer experience. Ergonomic chairs not only contribute to the comfort of clients during nail treatments but also support the posture and well-being of technicians who spend prolonged periods seated.

In addition to these core pieces of equipment, ancillary tools such as UV lamps, nail drills, disposal containers, and specialized lighting fixtures should be carefully chosen to complement the primary equipment and facilitate a smooth workflow. Careful consideration of each item's functionality, quality, and adherence to industry regulations is essential in creating a professional and reputable nail salon.

Ultimately, by identifying and investing in essential equipment that aligns with your salon's vision and values, you can ensure the delivery of exceptional nail services while fostering a safe and comfortable environment for both your clients and employees.

Evaluating Suppliers and Manufacturers

To ensure the success and efficiency of a nail salon business, evaluating suppliers and manufacturers is crucial when sourcing equipment and furniture. This process involves meticulous research and scrutiny to identify reputable and reliable partners in the industry. The selection of suppliers and manufacturers should be based on various factors such as product quality, pricing, reliability, and customer service.

When evaluating potential suppliers, consider their experience and reputation within the industry. Look for companies with a proven track record of delivering high-quality salon equipment and furniture. Researching customer reviews and seeking recommendations from other salon owners can provide valuable insights into the supplier's reliability and the satisfaction of their clients.

Consider the geographical location of suppliers and manufacturers as it can impact delivery times, shipping costs, and overall convenience. Local suppliers may offer advantages in terms of quicker delivery and easier communication, while international manufacturers might provide cost-effective options for bulk purchases.

Assessing the technical specifications and certifications of equipment offered by suppliers is imperative. Verify compliance with safety standards and regulations to ensure that the products meet industry requirements. Additionally, inquire about warranty policies, maintenance services, and after-sales support to gauge the level of commitment to customer satisfaction.

Comparing pricing structures from different suppliers is essential to make informed decisions. While cost-effectiveness is important, prioritize quality and reliability to avoid potential issues in the long run. Negotiating favorable payment terms and exploring package deals can also positively impact the procurement process.

Establish clear communication channels with selected suppliers and maintain open dialogue throughout the procurement process. Clear and precise documentation of agreements, including delivery schedules, payment terms, and return policies, is essential to avoid misunderstandings.

Ultimately, selecting the right suppliers and manufacturers for salon equipment and furniture is a strategic decision with far-reaching impacts on the operational efficiency and quality of the nail salon business. Diligent evaluation and selection of partners who align with the business's standards and goals will contribute to a streamlined procurement process and the establishment of a competitive edge in the industry.

Understanding Equipment Specifications

When sourcing equipment and furniture for a nail salon, understanding equipment specifications is paramount to making informed decisions. Equipment specifications encompass a range of technical details that outline the features, dimensions, capacity, and performance of the machinery and tools required in the salon setting. These specifications serve as the blueprint for selecting equipment that aligns with the salon's operational needs and quality standards.

One fundamental aspect of understanding equipment specifications involves comprehending the intricacies of each piece of equipment. This includes delving into factors such as power requirements, installation prerequisites, material compatibility, and usage instructions. Furthermore, examining the technical data related to the equipment's functionality, durability, and safety features is crucial in ensuring that the selected equipment meets industry regulations and safety standards.

Another pivotal component of equipment specifications pertains to assessing the ergonomic design and user interface. The ease of operation, ergonomics, and accessibility features of the equipment can significantly impact the overall efficiency and comfort of salon staff, thereby influencing productivity and customer experience. Evaluating these specifications enables salon owners to optimize workflow processes and create a conducive working environment for employees.

Moreover, scrutinizing the performance metrics outlined in the equipment specifications is essential for gauging the equipment's capability to meet the salon's demands. Specifications detailing parameters like speed, precision, noise levels, energy efficiency, and maintenance requirements play a pivotal role in determining the suitability of the equipment for the salon's intended use, anticipated workload, and space constraints.

In essence, understanding equipment specifications empowers salon owners to make informed decisions based on detailed technical insights. By carefully examining and comparing the specifications of various equipment options, salon proprietors can strategically select equipment that aligns with their budget, operational requirements, and long-term business objectives. Therefore, delving into the nuanced details presented in equipment specifications is a critical step in the procurement process, ensuring that the chosen equipment seamlessly integrates into the salon's operations while delivering optimal performance and value.

Calculating Equipment Costs

In the nail salon industry, calculating equipment costs is a crucial aspect of establishing a new business or expanding an existing one. The process involves a comprehensive assessment of the required equipment, from nail stations and pedicure chairs to UV lamps and ventilation systems. To begin with, it is essential to create a detailed inventory of all necessary equipment items, including their specifications, such as size, power requirements, and special features. Once the inventory is established, research and comparison of prices from various suppliers and manufacturers become imperative. This involves analyzing costs based on the quality, brand reputation, and additional functionalities offered by each equipment item. Moreover, factoring in shipping and installation expenses is critical to derive a complete picture of the total equipment investment. Furthermore, anticipating any potential customization or modification needs for specific equipment to meet operational requirements should be considered. Additionally, understanding the impact of currency fluctuations and market trends on equipment costs is essential for budgeting purposes. It is important to account for possible price variations during procurement to avoid unforeseen financial constraints. Furthermore, leveraging economies of scale through bulk purchases or establishing partnerships with equipment suppliers can lead to cost savings. Lastly, integrating the equipment costs into the overall budget and financial projections will provide a clear understanding of the capital required and assist in securing necessary funding. Ultimately, meticulous calculation of equipment costs is essential to ensure that the nail salon is equipped with high-quality, functional, and economically feasible equipment to support its operations and long-term success.

Assessing Warranty and Maintenance Services

In the nail salon industry, assessing warranty and maintenance services for equipment and furniture is vital to ensure operational continuity and cost-effectiveness. Warranty provisions vary across suppliers and manufacturers, warranting a comprehensive evaluation of coverage duration, terms, and conditions. When procuring equipment, meticulously scrutinizing the warranty details is imperative. This includes identifying the duration of coverage, which may range from months to years, and understanding the extent of protection offered for different components. Moreover, comprehending the terms and conditions that could void the warranty is essential to prevent inadvertent breaches. Another critical aspect is analyzing the availability of maintenance services. Assessing whether the supplier offers regular maintenance schedules, on-site repair services, or access to replacement parts is crucial for minimizing downtime and preserving the longevity of the equipment. The level of technical support provided by the manufacturer or supplier should also be considered, ensuring prompt resolution of any operational issues. Furthermore, evaluating the reputation and reliability of the service provider is instrumental in gauging the efficacy of potential maintenance support. Additionally, comprehensively examining the warranty and maintenance documentation to understand consumer rights, procedures for filing claims, and limitations of liability can mitigate uncertainties and unplanned expenses. Incorporating these assessments into the equipment procurement process enhances operational preparedness, safeguards against unforeseen disruptions, and optimizes the lifecycle costs of the nail salon setup.

Arranging Delivery and Installation

Upon finalizing the selection of equipment and furniture for your nail salon, the crucial step of arranging delivery and installation requires meticulous attention to detail. This process involves coordinating with suppliers and manufacturers to ensure timely and efficient transportation of the items to your salon's location. With precision and care, the delivery and installation phase significantly impacts the operational readiness of your nail salon.

When organizing the delivery, it is essential to work closely with the suppliers to establish a clear timeline for shipment and installation. Communication regarding delivery dates, potential delays, and handling procedures should be thorough and ongoing to prevent any logistical setbacks. Prior to the scheduled delivery, it is recommended to prepare the salon space to facilitate a smooth installation process. Adequate access for unloading, clear pathways, and designated installation areas should be arranged to expedite the process.

The next critical aspect is overseeing the installation itself. Collaborating with experienced installation professionals is imperative to guarantee the proper setup of equipment and furniture. Regular inspections during the installation process can help identify any discrepancies and address them promptly. It is also advisable to maintain open lines of communication with the installation team to address any unforeseen challenges that may arise. Moreover, adherence to safety protocols and installation guidelines provided by the manufacturers is paramount to ensure the functional integrity of the salon's equipment and furniture.

During this phase, documenting the delivery and installation process comprehensively is recommended. Taking photographs or videos of the unpacking, placement, and installation of each item can serve as valuable reference points in case of future inquiries or issues. Furthermore, maintaining detailed records of the delivery receipts, installation agreements, and warranty documentation can aid in streamlining post-installation support and servicing activities.

As the delivery and installation phase nears its completion, conducting thorough testing and quality checks on all installed equipment and furniture is vital. Functionality assessments, stability tests, and aesthetic evaluations should be conducted to ensure that each component meets the pre-established standards. Additionally, confirming that all parts, accessories, and accompanying manuals are accounted for and properly stored adds an extra layer of assurance for the salon's operational preparedness.

Ultimately, proficiently managing the process of delivery and installation contributes to the successful establishment of a well-equipped and functional nail salon. By meticulously overseeing these pivotal tasks, you optimize the initial operational efficiency and provide a solid foundation for delivering exceptional service to your clientele.

Ensuring Compliance with Industry Standards

In the nail salon industry, adherence to industry standards is paramount to ensure the safety and well-being of both clients and employees. Complying with regulations and guidelines set forth by regulatory bodies such as the Occupational Safety and Health Administration (OSHA), the Environmental Protection Agency (EPA), and state/local health departments is integral for obtaining and maintaining operational licenses.   When it comes to hygiene practices and sanitation protocols, nail salons must strictly adhere to regulations to prevent the spread of infections and ensure a clean, safe environment for clients. This involves implementing stringent procedures for sterilization of tools, disinfection of surfaces, and proper waste disposal. Additionally, ensuring that staff members receive adequate training on these protocols is crucial in maintaining compliance.   Furthermore, equipment used in nail salons must adhere to specific industry standards to guarantee quality and safety. This includes but is not limited to, manicure and pedicure stations, ventilation systems, and chemical storage. Implementing ergonomic design principles and utilizing materials that are easy to clean and maintain not only ensures compliance but also contributes to a comfortable and efficient working environment.   It is important for salon owners and managers to stay abreast of any changes or updates in industry standards, which may involve attending workshops, participating in webinars, or seeking guidance from industry associations. Regular inspections and audits can also help in identifying areas of improvement and rectifying any potential compliance issues.   Ultimately, prioritizing compliance with industry standards not only instills trust and confidence in clients but also mitigates legal and financial risks. By upholding these standards, nail salon owners demonstrate their commitment to professionalism, safety, and ethical business practices, setting them apart as reputable establishments within the competitive beauty industry.

Integrating Technology in Equipment Selection

In the modern nail salon industry, integrating technology in equipment selection has become a crucial aspect of setting up a successful salon. Advancements in technology have revolutionized the types of equipment available and the ways in which they can enhance the overall salon experience for both customers and technicians. When considering equipment selection, salon owners must carefully evaluate the technological features offered by various suppliers and manufacturers to ensure that their choices align with the salon's operational needs and provide a competitive edge in the market.

One of the primary considerations when integrating technology in equipment selection is the incorporation of smart devices and digital interfaces. For instance, the use of smart LED lamps for gel curing not only ensures efficient and precise curing of nail enhancements but also contributes to energy conservation. Furthermore, advanced manicure and pedicure stations equipped with integrated touch-screen controls offer an enhanced client experience by allowing customization of massage settings and nail treatment programs. In addition, the utilization of technology-driven ventilation systems and air purifiers helps maintain a clean and healthy salon environment, addressing concerns about air quality and sanitation.

Another significant aspect of technology integration in equipment selection pertains to the implementation of software solutions for managing appointments, inventory, and customer preferences. Salon management software enables streamlined scheduling, inventory tracking, and personalized client profiles, contributing to operational efficiency and improved customer satisfaction. Moreover, the integration of point-of-sale (POS) systems with secure payment processing capabilities not only facilitates convenient transactions but also enhances data security and financial transparency.

Furthermore, the use of advanced ergonomic design principles and material innovations in equipment manufacturing has been enabled by technological advancements. For example, the incorporation of 3D scanning and printing technologies allows for the creation of customized salon furniture and equipment tailored to specific spatial requirements and aesthetic preferences. Additionally, the application of virtual reality (VR) and augmented reality (AR) technologies offers salon owners and designers the ability to visualize and simulate different layouts and configurations before making final decisions, thus optimizing space utilization and enhancing the overall salon ambiance.

In conclusion, integrating technology in equipment selection is pivotal to the success of a modern nail salon. By leveraging the latest technological advancements, salon owners can elevate the quality of services, streamline operations, and create a unique and compelling salon environment that resonates with contemporary consumer expectations. It is essential for salon entrepreneurs to stay informed about emerging technologies and industry trends to make informed decisions that align with their business goals and contribute to long-term success.

Optimizing Furniture Layout and Selection

When establishing a nail salon, the furniture layout and selection play a crucial role in creating an inviting and functional environment for both clients and technicians. Optimal furniture layout not only enhances the overall aesthetic appeal of the salon but also contributes to efficient workflow and client comfort. The key to successful furniture optimization lies in understanding the spatial constraints, ergonomic requirements, and design coherence.

To begin with, thorough spatial analysis is essential to determine the ideal furniture arrangement. Factors such as traffic flow, operational zones, and accessibility need to be carefully considered. This involves mapping out the areas designated for manicure and pedicure stations, reception desk, waiting area, storage, and staff amenities. By strategically placing these elements, the layout can facilitate smooth movement within the salon while ensuring privacy and comfort for clients.

Furthermore, ergonomic considerations are paramount in furniture selection to prioritize the well-being of both clients and technicians. Ergonomically designed chairs, tables, and workstations promote proper posture and reduce the risk of physical strain or fatigue during extended periods of use. Adequate cushioning, adjustable height features, and ample legroom should be factored into the selection of furniture to guarantee optimal support and comfort for clientele and staff alike.

Design coherence is another vital aspect of furniture optimization that harmonizes the salon's ambiance and brand identity. Consistency in style, color scheme, and material selection across different furniture pieces ensures a cohesive visual presentation. Additionally, integrating elements of branding and thematic decor add a personalized touch that resonates with the salon's target demographic. Thoughtful consideration of these design elements contributes to a holistic and aesthetically pleasing environment that elevates the overall client experience.

In conclusion, the meticulous approach to optimizing furniture layout and selection is pivotal in shaping the functionality and ambiance of a nail salon. By addressing spatial, ergonomic, and design aspects, salon owners can curate an environment that fosters both operational efficiency and client satisfaction. Ultimately, the strategic integration of furniture within the salon space is instrumental in realizing a cohesive, welcoming, and operationally effective establishment.

Budgeting for Equipment and Furniture

Optimizing the allocation of financial resources for the procurement of equipment and furniture is pivotal to the successful establishment and operation of a nail salon. This section will comprehensively explore the intricate process of budgeting, encompassing the initial assessment of capital requirements, cost estimation, and strategic allocation of funds to ensure the seamless acquisition of essential assets. Beginning with an in-depth analysis of equipment and furniture needs, astute evaluation of available capital and projected revenue streams is imperative. It necessitates a judicious approach that considers factors such as scalability, quality, and longevity, aligning investments with the overarching vision for the salon while mitigating unnecessary expenditure. Proper budget allocation entails diligent research into the myriad options available in the market, juxtaposing the cost against the utility and lifespan of potential purchases. Moreover, it involves factoring in ancillary expenses such as delivery charges, installation fees, and warranty costs, thereby providing a holistic perspective on the total outlay. Efficient budgeting extends beyond mere cost estimation; it involves forecasting future operational expenditures and identifying opportunities for cost optimization that can potentially enhance the financial viability of the business. Engaging in negotiations with suppliers and leveraging bulk-purchase advantages are integral strategies and often demand a thorough comprehension of prevailing market rates and industry benchmarks. Furthermore, an adaptable budgeting framework can accommodate unforeseen contingencies, fostering resilience against fluctuations in pricing, thus safeguarding the financial health of the enterprise. Additionally, by incorporating metrics for return on investment (ROI) and lifetime value (LTV), prudent budgeting ensures that every procurement decision aligns with both short-term financial prudence and long-term sustainability. Recognizing the capital-intensive nature of the nail salon industry, this chapter explores methodologies for securing advantageous financing arrangements and maximizing purchasing power through lease and installment schemes, empowering entrepreneurs to capitalize on cutting-edge equipment and ergonomic furniture without succumbing to undue fiscal strain.

Quickreads Presents:: Open Your Own Nail Salon

Obtaining Necessary Certifications

Identifying Required Certifications

In the nail salon industry, identifying required certifications is a critical aspect of ensuring legal compliance and maintaining operational integrity. This process involves conducting comprehensive research to determine the specific certifications and credentials needed to operate a nail salon business within a particular jurisdiction. The identification of required certifications necessitates diligent investigation into local, state, and federal regulations pertaining to the beauty and personal care industry. Understanding the nuanced differences in regulations across various geographic areas is fundamental in this pursuit. To effectively identify these certifications, it is essential to engage with relevant regulatory bodies, such as health departments, licensing boards, and professional associations. These entities can provide invaluable insights into the exact certifications that are mandatory for operating a nail salon. Additionally, seeking guidance from experienced industry professionals and legal advisors can offer clarity on the intricacies of certification requirements. A methodical approach to this task involves creating a systematic checklist of all potential certifications, including those related to hygiene, sanitation, employee training, and business operation. Furthermore, staying abreast of any updates or changes to regulatory standards is crucial, as non-compliance can lead to severe penalties and jeopardize the success of the business. Identifying required certifications demands meticulous attention to detail and a commitment to upholding industry best practices, ultimately contributing to the establishment of a reputable and legally compliant nail salon.

Understanding Regulatory Standards

In the nail salon industry, understanding and adhering to regulatory standards are paramount for ensuring compliance and sustaining a safe working environment. Regulatory standards encompass a wide array of legal requirements, guidelines, and protocols established by federal, state, and local government agencies as well as industry organizations. These standards aim to safeguard the health and well-being of both employees and clients, and failure to comply can lead to severe penalties, reputation damage, and even business closure.

Comprehensive knowledge of applicable regulatory standards is essential for salon owners and staff. This includes familiarity with occupational safety and health regulations, sanitation requirements, licensing obligations, and other pertinent laws specific to the industry. Staying informed about any updates or changes in these standards is also crucial, as non-compliance can result from outdated practices.

To ensure adherence to these standards, salon owners must proactively monitor and evaluate their operations for compliance. This may involve conducting regular inspections, maintaining accurate records, and implementing corrective measures when necessary. Furthermore, developing internal policies and training programs that align with regulatory standards can promote a culture of compliance within the salon.

Collaborating with legal advisors or consultants proficient in regulatory matters can provide salon owners with valuable guidance in navigating the complexities of these standards. It is imperative to engage in continuous education and awareness-building regarding regulatory standards to mitigate potential risks and liabilities.

By delving into the intricate details of regulatory standards, salon owners can create a foundation that promotes operational excellence, upholds professional integrity, and fosters trust with clientele. Understanding and embracing regulatory standards not only positions the salon for sustainable success but also contributes to elevating industry standards across the board.

Navigating Health and Safety Guidelines

The provision of nail salon services necessitates a comprehensive understanding and adherence to health and safety guidelines. Navigating these guidelines is essential to ensure the well-being of both clientele and staff members. Health and safety guidelines encompass a spectrum of considerations, including sanitation protocols, chemical exposure mitigation, ergonomic practices, and infection control measures. Salon owners and technicians must be well-versed in OSHA regulations, state-specific guidelines, and industry best practices. They are responsible for implementing these guidelines to guarantee a secure and hygienic environment within the salon premises. Understanding the potential risks and hazards associated with nail salon procedures is paramount. This encompasses recognizing the dangers of exposure to hazardous chemicals present in products such as polishes, solvents, and disinfectants. Nail technicians must be trained to handle chemicals safely and employ protective measures to minimize occupational health risks.

Moreover, the ergonomic layout of the salon must be meticulously planned to reduce the likelihood of muscular-skeletal injuries among staff. Proper ventilation systems should be in place to mitigate inhalation of fumes, and comprehensive hygiene practices are crucial to prevent the transmission of infectious diseases. Adhering to health and safety guidelines necessitates ongoing education and awareness. Technicians should stay abreast of updates in sanitation and hygiene practices, while salon owners must consistently audit their establishments to ensure compliance with the latest standards. Navigating health and safety guidelines demands dedication and vigilance. By prioritizing these measures, nail salons can create a safe and welcoming environment for both employees and clients.

Securing Sanitary Permits

Sanitary permits play a crucial role in ensuring the safety and well-being of both employees and clients within a nail salon establishment. These permits are typically issued by local health departments or regulatory agencies, and their attainment is vital for maintaining a clean and hygienic environment. To secure sanitary permits, salon owners must adhere to stringent guidelines pertaining to sanitation, sterilization, and cleanliness. The process usually begins with a thorough assessment of the salon's facilities, equipment, and operational procedures. This involves a comprehensive review of waste disposal methods, disinfection protocols, and infection control measures. Additionally, the layout and maintenance of the salon space must align with established sanitary standards. Aspects such as ventilation systems and plumbing fixtures are scrutinized to optimize air quality and prevent potential health hazards. Furthermore, documentation of cleaning schedules and product usage is imperative to demonstrate compliance with sanitary regulations. Following this, salon operators must undergo education and training on best practices for maintaining a sanitized environment. This includes understanding proper hand hygiene, surface disinfection, and the handling of hazardous materials. Training programs often cover topics such as bloodborne pathogens, chemical safety, and the prevention of cross-contamination. Once the necessary preparations and training have been completed, a formal application for the sanitary permit can be submitted to the relevant authority. This typically entails providing detailed records of compliance with regulatory requirements, as well as evidence of staff education and facility maintenance. Inspections may be conducted to verify adherence to regulations before the permit is issued. After securing the sanitary permit, ongoing vigilance is essential to uphold the established standards. Regular self-assessments and audits should be conducted to ensure continued compliance with sanitary regulations, and any necessary corrective actions should be promptly implemented. Overall, the acquisition and maintenance of sanitary permits are fundamental components of operating a responsible and reputable nail salon that prioritizes the health and safety of its patrons and staff.

Obtaining Professional Licenses

In the nail salon industry, obtaining professional licenses is a critical aspect of ensuring compliance and credibility. Professional licenses serve as an official acknowledgment of an individual's qualifications and skills in providing nail care services. This section explores the detailed process of acquiring these licenses and the significance they hold within the industry.

Professional licenses for nail technicians typically involve fulfilling specific educational requirements and completing examinations to demonstrate proficiency. These requirements are often established by state regulatory bodies or licensing boards to guarantee that practitioners possess the necessary knowledge and expertise to perform their duties safely and effectively. Moreover, obtaining a professional license involves adhering to ethical standards and regulations set forth by the governing authorities, emphasizing the commitment to maintaining professionalism and ethical conduct within the profession.

The process of obtaining these licenses begins with enrolling in accredited nail technician programs that align with the regulatory standards and curriculum outlined by the licensing board. These programs provide comprehensive training on various aspects of nail care, including sanitation protocols, infection control practices, nail art techniques, and customer service skills. Upon successful completion of the educational requirements, aspiring nail technicians must sit for rigorous licensing examinations, which evaluate their theoretical knowledge and practical abilities in performing nail treatments and procedures.

Additionally, applicants are required to submit documentation, such as proof of education, training hours, and background checks, to support their license applications. These documents serve as evidence of the individual's eligibility and qualification to practice as a licensed nail technician. Furthermore, candidates may need to fulfill additional criteria, such as CPR certification and first aid training, to ensure readiness in handling emergency situations at the salon.

Upon meeting all prerequisites and passing the licensure examinations, individuals become eligible to apply for their professional nail technician licenses. The application process entails submitting the necessary forms, fees, and supporting documentation to the respective licensing board for review and approval. Once granted, the professional license empowers nail technicians to legally offer their services, build their clientele, and contribute to the reputable image of the nail salon industry.

It is essential for nail salon owners and managers to recognize the significance of employing licensed professionals, as it reflects the commitment to upholding industry standards and prioritizing the well-being of clients. By ensuring that all staff members hold valid professional licenses, nail salons can cultivate a culture of professionalism, trust, and excellence, thereby enhancing their competitive position in the market and fostering long-term client relationships.

Meeting Industry-specific Requirements

The nail salon industry is subject to various industry-specific requirements that are essential for ensuring compliance and maintaining high-quality standards. These requirements encompass a broad range of factors, including but not limited to product usage, sanitation protocols, employee training, and customer safety. This section will delve into the critical aspects of meeting industry-specific requirements within the nail salon business.

One fundamental aspect of meeting industry-specific requirements is the meticulous selection and utilization of nail products and materials. Nail salons must adhere to strict guidelines when it comes to using and storing chemicals, polishes, and other nail care products. Understanding the composition of these products, their potential hazards, and proper handling procedures is paramount in meeting industry-specific requirements.

Additionally, maintaining optimal hygiene and sanitation practices is imperative in the nail salon industry. Compliance with industry-specific standards involves implementing rigorous cleaning and disinfection protocols for tools, equipment, and workspaces. Establishing comprehensive cleanliness procedures helps prevent the spread of infections and ensures a safe environment for both employees and clients.

Furthermore, adhering to industry-specific training requirements is vital for the professional development of nail salon staff. From mastering advanced nail techniques to understanding customer service best practices, ongoing training plays a pivotal role in meeting industry-specific requirements. Employing knowledgeable and skilled technicians not only enhances the salon's reputation but also contributes to the overall quality of service provided.

Another critical element is maintaining customer safety through the implementation of specific procedures and protocols. This may include conducting skin tests prior to certain treatments, adhering to age restrictions for certain services, and providing accurate information on potential risks and aftercare. By strictly following industry-specific requirements related to customer safety, nail salons can foster a culture of trust and reliability among their clientele.

In conclusion, meeting industry-specific requirements in the nail salon business demands unwavering dedication to excellence, attention to detail, and a thorough understanding of the unique standards and expectations within the industry. Successfully aligning with these requirements not only fosters regulatory compliance but also elevates the overall standing of the business within the competitive market.

Conducting Inspections and Audits

Conducting regular inspections and audits is an integral aspect of maintaining compliance within the nail salon industry. These processes are designed to ensure that the salon meets all regulatory standards, health and safety guidelines, and industry-specific requirements. Inspections may be conducted by government agencies, such as the Health Department or

Occupational Safety and Health Administration (OSHA), as well as by independent auditors hired by the salon. It is imperative for salon owners and managers to proactively prepare for these evaluations.

The first step in conducting inspections and audits is to establish a comprehensive checklist based on relevant regulations and industry best practices. This checklist should cover all aspects of the salon's operations, including hygiene protocols, equipment maintenance, chemical handling, ventilation systems, staff training records, and client consent forms. The checklist serves as a guideline for both internal self-assessments and external audits.

During inspections, salon personnel must cooperate fully with the inspectors, providing them with access to all areas of the facility and necessary documentation. It is important to remain transparent and forthcoming with information to demonstrate a commitment to compliance. Inspectors will evaluate the salon's adherence to standards regarding sanitation, sterilization, cleanliness, and overall occupational health and safety. Any deviations from the established norms may result in citations, fines, or closure orders, making it vital to address any deficiencies promptly.

Moreover, audits, whether conducted internally or by third-party professionals, are essential for identifying any non-compliance issues and implementing corrective actions. Through audits, salon management can assess the effectiveness of their compliance procedures, identify potential risks, and improve operational protocols. It is crucial to document all audit findings and develop a remediation plan to address areas of concern. Integrating the recommendations from audits into regular staff training and procedural updates can facilitate continuous improvement within the salon.

In summary, conducting inspections and audits requires meticulous preparation, unwavering adherence to regulations, and a proactive approach to addressing any shortcomings. By diligently performing these evaluations, salon owners and managers can maintain a safe, hygienic, and compliant environment for both their employees and clients.

Documenting Compliance Procedures

In the nail salon industry, documenting compliance procedures is vital for ensuring adherence to licensing regulations, health and safety guidelines, and industry standards. Thorough documentation serves as a record of the salon's commitment to maintaining a safe and hygienic environment for both clients and staff. This section will elucidate the essential aspects of documenting compliance procedures, emphasizing the significance of meticulous record-keeping and the seamless integration of compliance documentation into the salon's operational framework.

Documentation of compliance procedures begins with a comprehensive understanding of the regulatory requirements governing the nail salon sector. It entails identifying the specific certifications, permits, licenses, and standards that are pertinent to the operation of a nail salon. Whether it pertains to sanitation protocols, ventilation systems, or hazardous waste disposal, each aspect must be meticulously documented to demonstrate adherence to the prescribed norms.

Moreover, employing standardized templates and forms designed for documentation aids in streamlining the process. These templates can encompass checklists for routine inspections, logs for equipment maintenance, and training records for staff. Furthermore, digitalizing documentation through specialized software not only ensures efficient record-keeping but also facilitates easy retrieval and analysis of compliance data.

Additionally, it is imperative to establish a systematic procedure for updating and archiving compliance documentation. Regular reviews and revisions of documented procedures enable the salon to adapt to evolving regulatory requirements and technological advancements. Designating responsible personnel for overseeing the documentation process fosters accountability and ensures that records are current and accurate.

Furthermore, effective documentation of compliance procedures serves as a valuable resource during audits and inspections. It enables regulatory authorities to assess the salon's adherence to industry regulations and validates the salon's commitment to maintaining high standards of hygiene and safety. Thoroughly documented procedures not only demonstrate legal compliance but also instill confidence in clients, portraying the salon as a reputable establishment committed to excellence.

In conclusion, documenting compliance procedures is a cornerstone of regulatory compliance and operational excellence in the nail salon industry. By meticulously recording adherence to regulatory standards, maintaining up-to-date documentation, and integrating compliance records into everyday operations, a nail salon can ensure a safe, hygienic, and legally compliant environment. Through comprehensive documentation, a salon can uphold its reputation, instill trust in clients, and demonstrate unwavering dedication to the well-being of its patrons and employees.

Implementing Ongoing Training Programs

In the nail salon industry, implementing ongoing training programs is essential for ensuring that all staff members are equipped with the necessary skills and knowledge to adhere to regulatory standards and provide high-quality services. These training programs should encompass a wide range of topics, including hygiene practices, safety protocols, customer service standards, and industry trends. It is imperative to establish a structured training curriculum that addresses both theoretical knowledge and practical skills. By incorporating a comprehensive approach to training, salon owners can cultivate a culture of continuous learning and improvement within their team.

The first step in implementing ongoing training programs is to conduct a thorough assessment of the specific training needs within the salon. This involves identifying areas where further skill development or knowledge enhancement is required. Based on this assessment, a tailored training plan can be developed to address these identified needs. This plan should outline the objectives of each training module, the intended learning outcomes, the methods of delivery, and the assessment criteria. Moreover, it should specify the frequency of training sessions and the responsible parties for conducting and overseeing the training activities.

Once the training plan has been established, it is crucial to allocate adequate resources to support its implementation. This includes providing access to relevant training materials, securing training facilities or equipment, and allocating time for employees to participate in training activities without negatively impacting daily operations. Furthermore, it may be beneficial to leverage external expertise or specialized trainers to deliver certain aspects of the training program, especially for advanced techniques or industry-specific subjects.

Effective training programs also necessitate the use of diverse instructional methods to cater to different learning styles and preferences. Incorporating interactive workshops, practical demonstrations, role-playing scenarios, and multimedia presentations can enhance the engagement and retention of information among the staff. Additionally, encouraging participation in industry conferences, workshops, and webinars can expose employees to the latest trends and best practices, contributing to their professional growth and development.

Evaluation and feedback mechanisms should be integrated into the ongoing training programs to measure the effectiveness of the training initiatives. Regular assessments, quizzes, and observations can gauge the level of understanding and skill proficiency attained by the employees. Feedback from both trainers and trainees should be welcomed to identify areas for improvement and ensure that the training content remains relevant and impactful.

Ultimately, ongoing training programs should be viewed as an investment in the salon's success and the professional development of its employees. By prioritizing continuous learning and skill enhancement, nail salon owners can cultivate a team of competent and knowledgeable professionals who uphold the highest standards of service and regulatory compliance. This commitment to ongoing training not only benefits the salon internally, but also contributes to building a positive reputation and fostering long-term customer satisfaction.

Developing a Compliance Maintenance Plan

In the nail salon industry, compliance with regulations and standards is paramount to ensuring the safety of both employees and clients. Developing a comprehensive compliance maintenance plan is essential for upholding these standards and fostering a culture of continuous improvement within the salon. This plan involves proactive measures to sustain adherence to all necessary certifications and regulations, thereby mitigating the risk of violations and potential reputational damage.

The first step in developing a compliance maintenance plan is to conduct an in-depth review of all relevant regulations and certifications applicable to the nail salon business. This includes federal, state, and local regulations covering areas such as sanitation, hygiene, employee training, and workplace safety. By identifying the specific requirements that apply to the salon, owners and managers can systematically outline the necessary steps for compliance.

Once the regulatory landscape has been thoroughly assessed, the next phase focuses on establishing protocols for regular internal audits and inspections. This involves designating responsible employees or teams to carry out routine assessments of the salon's adherence to regulatory standards. These internal evaluations aim to identify any areas of non-compliance and address them promptly through corrective actions.

Furthermore, a crucial aspect of the compliance maintenance plan lies in the documentation of all compliance-related activities. This includes record-keeping for inspections, training sessions, certification renewals, and any corrective measures taken. Maintaining detailed records not only serves as evidence of compliance but also facilitates transparency during external audits or inquiries.

As part of the compliance maintenance plan, it's imperative to institute a culture of continuous learning and improvement among salon staff. This involves providing ongoing education and training on evolving regulations, best practices, and new technologies or products entering the market. By keeping employees well-informed and equipped with the latest knowledge, salons can proactively adapt to changes and uphold the highest standards of compliance.

To ensure the successful implementation of the compliance maintenance plan, regular management reviews and updates are essential. This involves periodic evaluations of the plan's effectiveness, adjustments in response to regulatory changes, and opportunities for feedback from employees. Additionally, leveraging technology solutions, such as compliance management software, can streamline the monitoring and reporting of compliance activities.

Ultimately, a robust compliance maintenance plan forms the cornerstone of a reputable and trustworthy nail salon business. By prioritizing compliance, not only does the salon uphold ethical and legal responsibilities, but it also conveys a commitment to professionalism and customer well-being. With a holistic approach to compliance maintenance, the salon can enhance its competitive edge and foster a loyal clientele who value a safe and compliant environment for their beauty and grooming needs.

Quickreads Presents:: Open Your Own Nail Salon

Designing Aesthetic Layouts

Analyzing Space Utilization

Analyzing space utilization in a nail salon is a critical aspect of the design process. It involves the strategic assessment of how the available space can be optimally utilized to create an efficient and aesthetically pleasing layout. To begin this analysis, it is essential to conduct a thorough examination of the dimensions and configuration of the salon. This includes assessing the spatial characteristics such as floor area, ceiling height, and any architectural features that may impact the layout.

The next step is to evaluate the functional requirements of the salon. This encompasses determining the specific zones within the space, such as reception areas, workstations, washing stations, and storage areas. Each zone needs to be carefully considered in terms of its purpose and the flow of activity within the salon. Understanding the operational workflow and client journey is pivotal in ensuring that the space is utilized in an ergonomic and efficient manner.

Furthermore, the analysis should address the integration of essential amenities and equipment within the space. This involves identifying the placement of fixtures, such as manicure and pedicure stations, treatment beds, and nail drying stations, to facilitate a smooth and organized service delivery process. Additionally, considerations must be made for accommodating necessary facilities like sinks, storage units, and employee workstations.

In parallel with these assessments, it is crucial to take into account the aesthetic aspects of the space. Balancing functionality with visual appeal is fundamental in creating an inviting and comfortable environment for both clients and staff. Therefore, the analysis of space utilization should also encompass evaluating opportunities for incorporating elements of decor, branding, and ambiance to enhance the overall atmosphere of the salon.

Ultimately, analyzing space utilization demands a holistic approach that integrates practical, operational, and design considerations. By undertaking this comprehensive evaluation, salon owners and designers can make informed decisions that result in an optimized layout conducive to delivering exceptional services, maximizing productivity, and fostering a memorable experience for clientele.

Selecting Ergonomic Furniture

In the nail salon industry, selecting ergonomic furniture is crucial to ensure the comfort and well-being of both clients and staff. Ergonomic furniture is designed to support the body in a way that minimizes the risk of musculoskeletal disorders and maximizes productivity. When choosing ergonomic furniture for a nail salon, various factors must be taken into consideration. Firstly, the selection process should begin with an assessment of the specific tasks that will be performed while seated at the furniture, such as manicures, pedicures, and nail art. Understanding the range of motions and postures required for these tasks is essential in determining the optimal ergonomic features needed in the furniture. Additionally, the design and material of the furniture play a critical role in ensuring comfort and durability. The furniture should allow for easy adjustment to accommodate different body sizes and preferences. Moreover, it should be constructed from high-quality materials that can withstand frequent use and sanitation procedures. Furthermore, integrating customizable elements, such as adjustable armrests and cushioned seating, can provide enhanced comfort and support. Considering the long hours often spent by nail technicians working with clients, investing in ergonomic furniture not only promotes their well-being but also contributes to a more professional and efficient salon environment. By prioritizing the selection of ergonomic furniture, salon owners can demonstrate their commitment to creating a space that prioritizes both the client experience and the health of their employees.

Optimizing Traffic Flow

Optimizing traffic flow within a nail salon is fundamental to creating an efficient and pleasant customer experience. The layout of a salon plays a crucial role in how customers move through the space, impacting their overall impression and satisfaction. To achieve an optimal traffic flow, several key factors must be taken into consideration. Firstly, the positioning of workstations and service areas should be strategically planned to minimize congestion and ensure a seamless transition for both customers and staff. This involves analyzing foot traffic patterns and implementing an intelligent layout that guides customers through the salon in an intuitive manner. Additionally, clear pathways and designated waiting areas help manage customer movement efficiently. Selecting appropriate flooring materials, such as non-slip surfaces, can contribute to safety and ease of navigation. Furthermore, optimizing traffic flow also involves considering accessibility and compliance with ADA regulations to accommodate customers with mobility challenges. By incorporating these principles, nail salon owners can create an environment that not only maximizes operational efficiency but also enhances the overall customer experience.

Integrating Brand Identity

In the nail salon industry, effectively integrating brand identity within the aesthetic layout is crucial to establishing a distinctive and cohesive image. This section will delve into the nuanced strategies and technical aspects of aligning the physical space with the overarching brand ethos.

Central to this integration is the deliberate selection of visual elements that encapsulate the brand's values and resonate with the target demographic. From color schemes to typography, every design choice should harmonize with the brand's narrative, creating a unified and immersive experience for clients. Moreover, incorporating brand logos and motifs into the salon's interior design subtly reinforces brand recognition and fosters a lasting impression.

A key technical consideration when integrating brand identity is the meticulous attention to detail required in material selection and finishings. The tactile and visual quality of materials such as flooring, furniture upholstery, and wall treatments should embody the brand's perceived craftsmanship and luxury. Additionally, leveraging effective signage and displays that reflect the brand's persona directly contributes to a coherent and impactful environment.

Furthermore, the utilization of technology can be harnessed to reinforce brand identity. This extends beyond digital displays and interactive features to encompass sensory experiences, where custom scents or soundscapes can be integrated to evoke specific brand associations, completing the holistic sensory branding approach.

The implementation of brand identity in the layout is not merely an aesthetic endeavor but also a strategic one. It influences consumer perception, fostering loyalty and differentiation in a competitive landscape. Through meticulously crafted and technically-informed integration, a nail salon can elevate its brand identity from a mere label to a compelling and memorable presence, resonating with clientele and setting itself apart as a benchmark of excellence.

Utilizing Effective Lighting Design

Effective lighting design is integral to the success of a nail salon as it contributes to the overall ambiance, customer experience, and operational efficiency. Properly utilized lighting can enhance the visual appeal of the salon, create a calming and inviting atmosphere, and highlight the salon's brand identity. Furthermore, it plays a vital role in ensuring compliance with safety and regulatory standards.

When designing the lighting layout for a nail salon, it is essential to consider both natural and artificial lighting sources. Natural light not only reduces the reliance on artificial lighting during the day but also provides a sense of openness and connection to the outdoors. Strategically positioning windows or incorporating skylights can optimize the use of natural light while minimizing glare and heat gain.

Artificial lighting should be carefully planned to achieve a balance between ambient, task, and accent lighting. Ambient lighting sets the overall tone and brightness of the space, creating a comfortable environment for both clients and technicians. Task lighting is crucial at individual workstations to ensure proper illumination for detailed nail treatments. Accent lighting, such as decorative fixtures or LED strips, can add visual interest and draw attention to specific areas or retail displays.

Incorporating energy-efficient lighting technologies, such as LED fixtures, not only reduces operational costs but also aligns with sustainability efforts. Additionally, utilizing dimmers and sensors can provide flexibility in controlling the intensity and timing of the lighting, catering to different service times and ambiance preferences.

Moreover, the selection of lighting fixtures should align with the brand image and interior design concept of the salon. Modern, sleek fixtures may complement contemporary salon designs, while ornate fixtures can enhance a more traditional or luxurious ambiance. Color temperature and color rendering index (CRI) of the light sources should also be considered to ensure accurate color representation and a flattering appearance of nail polishes and nail art.

From a regulatory perspective, compliance with building codes and occupational health and safety regulations is crucial in lighting design. Ensuring adequate illumination levels, especially in areas where chemical products are handled, contributes to a safe working environment. Properly shielded and enclosed light fixtures are essential to prevent potential hazards and mitigate risks associated with electrical components.

In summary, effective lighting design in a nail salon goes beyond aesthetics; it encompasses functionality, safety, and branding. By thoughtfully integrating natural and artificial lighting, selecting appropriate fixtures, and adhering to regulatory guidelines, a nail salon can elevate its overall appeal and provide a memorable experience for clients.

Incorporating Regulatory Compliance Measures

In the nail salon industry, compliance with regulatory requirements is paramount to ensure the safety and well-being of both clients and employees. Designing the aesthetic layout of a nail salon necessitates a thorough understanding and integration of various regulations to create a harmonious and compliant environment. Incorporating regulatory compliance measures involves adherence to zoning laws, building codes, fire safety regulations, and health and sanitation standards. Zoning laws dictate the permissible land usage for the nail salon, ensuring it is located in an appropriate area designated for commercial activities. Building codes outline structural requirements, ensuring that the salon space meets safety standards for construction, occupancy, and accessibility. Fire safety regulations mandate the installation of adequate fire suppression systems, smoke detectors, and emergency exits to safeguard against potential fire hazards. Health and sanitation standards encompass a wide range of requirements, including proper ventilation systems, sewage disposal, plumbing standards, and hazardous waste management. Adhering to these standards fosters a hygienic and safe environment, mitigating health risks and ensuring the well-being of all occupants within the salon. Failing to comply with these regulations can result in serious consequences such as fines, legal issues, or even closure of the business. Therefore, meticulous attention to detail and adherence to regulatory compliance measures are essential components of the design process for a nail salon, guaranteeing a secure and legally compliant establishment.

Leveraging Color Psychology

The strategic use of color psychology in a nail salon's aesthetic layout is crucial for creating an ambiance that resonates with clients on both a conscious and subconscious level. Understandably, colors have a profound impact on human emotions, behaviors, and perceptions, making them a powerful tool in shaping customer experiences. When applied properly, the psychological influence of colors can evoke desired feelings, such as relaxation, rejuvenation, or confidence, ultimately enhancing the overall atmosphere of the salon.

Incorporating color psychology begins with a comprehensive analysis of the target demographic and the intended emotional response. Warm hues, including shades of red, orange, and yellow, are known to stimulate energy and create a sense of warmth and intimacy. They can be strategically used in waiting areas or social spaces to encourage conversation and sociability. On the other hand, cool tones like blues, greens, and purples are often associated with tranquility, serenity, and trust, thus making them ideal for treatment rooms where clients seek relaxation and stress relief.

Furthermore, understanding cultural connotations of colors is pivotal, as interpretations vary across different demographics. For instance, while white symbolizes purity and cleanliness in some cultures, it may signify mourning or loss in others. This cultural sensitivity is vital when designing an inclusive and welcoming environment for a diverse clientele base.

When integrating color psychology, it is imperative to consider the overall visual harmony and balance within the space. Experimenting with complementary or analogous color schemes can create a cohesive and aesthetically pleasing environment. Additionally, the strategic application of accent colors can draw attention to specific focal points, such as retail displays or feature walls, thereby influencing customer behavior and promoting retail sales.

Educating staff members about the rationale behind the chosen color scheme can also enhance their understanding of the salon's branding and values, empowering them to deliver a consistent and immersive client experience. Furthermore, incorporating feedback mechanisms, such as client surveys or observations, can provide valuable insights into the effectiveness of the chosen color palette in eliciting the intended emotional responses.

In essence, leveraging color psychology in the nail salon's aesthetic layout entails a thoughtful and deliberate approach aimed at creating a sensory journey that resonates with clients. By harnessing the emotive power of colors, the salon can craft an environment that appeals to its target audience, fosters emotional connections, and elevates the overall customer experience.

Displaying Retail Products Strategically

In the nail salon industry, strategic product displays play a pivotal role in maximizing sales and enhancing the overall customer experience. When designing an aesthetic layout for retail products, it is crucial to consider various factors that can influence consumer behavior and purchasing decisions. Displaying retail products strategically involves a comprehensive approach that encompasses visual appeal, accessibility, and effective communication of product features and benefits. The layout should be designed with the goal of drawing attention, stimulating interest, and ultimately driving purchase intent.

One key aspect of displaying retail products strategically is the concept of visual hierarchy. This involves arranging products in a manner that guides the customer's focus towards specific items, promoting those with higher profit margins or seasonal relevance. Through thoughtful placement and grouping, the visual hierarchy can direct the customer's attention to featured products while still allowing visibility of the full range of offerings.

Endcaps and feature displays are effective tools for highlighting promotional items or new arrivals. By carefully curating these prominent areas, businesses can create a sense of urgency and excitement, prompting impulse purchases and boosting overall sales. Additionally, incorporating interactive elements such as demonstration stations or product testers can provide customers with hands-on experiences, further increasing engagement and fostering a deeper connection with the products.

Another critical consideration is the strategic use of signage and product information. Clear, concise signage contributes to the customer's understanding of the products, guiding them through their decision-making process. Thematic displays and story-driven setups can evoke emotion and create a narrative around the products, resulting in a more immersive and memorable shopping experience.

Furthermore, the thoughtful integration of sensory elements such as scents and music can elevate the ambiance and contribute to a cohesive brand experience. It's essential to ensure that the layout allows for easy navigation and intuitive product discovery. This can be achieved through well-defined pathways and logical categorization, enabling customers to explore the offerings while feeling confident and supported in their decision-making.

Ultimately, by strategically displaying retail products, nail salons can not only drive sales but also reinforce their brand identity and strengthen their competitive edge in the market. A meticulously planned and executed layout can create a lasting impression on customers, encouraging repeat visits and fostering loyalty. As the retail landscape continues to evolve, the ability to strategically display products will remain a cornerstone of successful nail salon businesses.

Implementing Visual Merchandising Techniques

Visual merchandising plays a crucial role in the success of a nail salon, as it directly influences the customer's perception of the salon's products and services. Implementing effective visual merchandising techniques involves a strategic approach to presenting retail products in an aesthetically pleasing and persuasive manner. The layout and design of the retail display area should be carefully planned to create an inviting atmosphere that encourages customers to explore and purchase items.

One key aspect of visual merchandising is creating visually compelling product displays. This involves utilizing various props, signage, and lighting to draw attention to featured products and highlight their unique selling points. By implementing principles of good design, such as balance, proportion, and focal points, nail salon owners can effectively showcase their retail inventory and drive sales.

Furthermore, an understanding of consumer behavior is essential when implementing visual merchandising techniques. By considering the target audience's preferences and purchasing habits, salon owners can tailor their product displays to resonate with their customers. For instance, if the target demographic prefers eco-friendly or luxury products, the visual merchandising should reflect those preferences through the selection of products and the display aesthetics.

In addition to crafting appealing product displays, the strategic placement of merchandise within the salon can significantly impact sales. Placing high-margin or new products at eye level and in high-traffic areas can increase their visibility and desirability, ultimately driving purchase intent. Moreover, seasonal promotions and themed displays can create excitement and encourage impulse buying.

To optimize the impact of visual merchandising, it is crucial to regularly assess and refresh the display arrangements. Rotating products, updating signage, and incorporating seasonal elements can help maintain a dynamic and engaging shopping environment that motivates customers to return and explore new offerings.

Finally, leveraging technology as part of visual merchandising can enhance the overall customer experience. Digital displays, interactive kiosks, or virtual reality experiences can captivate customers and provide them with valuable information about products and services. Integrating technology into the visual merchandising strategy demonstrates innovation and can set a salon apart from competitors.

By implementing effective visual merchandising techniques, nail salons can elevate the presentation of their retail products, stimulate customer interest, and ultimately drive sales and customer satisfaction.

Integrating Technology for Customer Experience

In the contemporary nail salon industry, integrating technology is essential to enhancing the overall customer experience. Advancements in technology have revolutionized the way customers interact with businesses, and nail salons are no exception. From online booking systems to digital nail design platforms, leveraging technology can significantly elevate customer satisfaction and loyalty.

One of the key aspects of integrating technology for customer experience is implementing a user-friendly and efficient online booking system. By providing clients with the convenience of scheduling appointments through a website or mobile app, salons can streamline the reservation process and offer greater flexibility to their clientele. Moreover, personalized appointment reminders and notifications can be automated through technology, reducing no-show rates and improving overall operational efficiency.

Furthermore, digital nail design platforms have become increasingly popular in modern nail salons. These tools enable customers to explore diverse nail art options digitally before making their selections, thereby enhancing the customization and personalization of their salon experience. Additionally, the integration of virtual reality (VR) or augmented reality (AR) technology can allow clients to visualize different nail designs in real-time, offering an interactive and immersive experience.

Another pivotal aspect of technological integration involves implementing customer relationship management (CRM) systems tailored to the nail salon industry. These systems can capture and analyze customer preferences and purchase history, enabling salons to provide tailored recommendations and personalized services, thereby fostering stronger client relationships.

Moreover, leveraging technology to offer multimedia entertainment options during services can enhance the overall customer experience. Integrated entertainment systems, such as streaming services or interactive displays, can provide clients with a more enjoyable and immersive environment, ultimately leading to higher satisfaction levels.

Integrating technology also includes embracing contactless payment solutions, which not only promote hygiene and safety but also contribute to expedited checkout processes, minimizing customer wait times and maximizing operational efficiency.

Ultimately, by effectively integrating technology for customer experience, nail salons can elevate service quality, boost customer satisfaction, and differentiate themselves in the competitive market, ultimately leading to long-term success and profitability.

Quickreads Presents:: Open Your Own Nail Salon

Implementing Hygiene Practices

Understanding Cleanliness Standards

Maintaining high cleanliness standards is imperative in the nail salon industry to ensure the well-being of both clients and employees. Understanding the nuances of cleanliness standards involves a deep dive into regulatory requirements, best practices, and the selection of appropriate sanitization products and equipment. Unquestionably, adherence to strict cleanliness standards not only fosters a safe and hygienic environment but also upholds the reputation and credibility of the salon. By comprehensively comprehending the fundamental principles of cleanliness, nail salon owners can cultivate trust and confidence among their clientele. This trust is built on the assurance that the salon prioritizes the health and safety of everyone who walks through its doors. Moreover, understanding cleanliness standards also involves staying abreast of emerging trends, innovations, and advancements in the field of sanitization and sterilization. By remaining informed, salon owners can proactively adapt their practices to align with the latest industry guidelines and technologies, thereby ensuring optimal cleanliness and hygiene. In this section, we will delve into the core concepts of cleanliness standards, covering topics such as the identification of regulatory mandates, the significance of quality sanitization products, and the integration of rigorous cleaning protocols. With a profound understanding of cleanliness standards, nail salon professionals can propel their establishments towards a culture of excellence in hygiene, setting them apart as industry leaders dedicated to the utmost care and well-being of their patrons.

Selecting Sanitization Products and Equipment

In the nail salon industry, the selection of sanitization products and equipment plays a pivotal role in maintaining the highest standards of hygiene and cleanliness. When choosing sanitization products, it is imperative to prioritize efficacy and compatibility with salon surfaces and materials. Antiseptic solutions, disinfectants, sanitizing wipes, and sterilization pouches are essential tools in the arsenal of a well-equipped nail salon. These products should be EPA-approved and designed to effectively eliminate bacteria, viruses, fungi, and other pathogens commonly encountered in salon environments.

Moreover, the selection of sanitization equipment such as autoclaves, UV sterilizers, and chemical sterilizers requires careful consideration. Autoclaves, for instance, are crucial for sterilizing metal implements and should comply with industry regulations. Understanding the maintenance requirements, capacity, and operational specifications of these devices is paramount to their effective utilization in upholding hygiene standards.

Additionally, the salon should invest in durable and functional cleaning equipment including hospital-grade cleaning solutions, brushes, and gloves. Investing in touchless dispensers for soaps and sanitizers can further minimize the risk of cross-contamination. It is indispensable for salon owners and managers to stay abreast of advancements in sanitization technology and continuously assess the efficacy of their chosen products and equipment.

Furthermore, establishing a robust inventory management system for sanitization products ensures that adequate stock is maintained at all times. Conducting regular audits to assess product expiration dates and replenishing supplies in a timely manner is vital to prevent lapses in sanitation practices. Emphasizing proper training for staff in the correct usage and application of sanitization products and equipment is essential to ensure consistency and thoroughness in maintaining hygiene protocols.

By giving meticulous attention to the selection of sanitization products and equipment, a nail salon can cultivate an environment that not only meets but exceeds industry cleanliness standards, ultimately instilling confidence in clients and setting a benchmark for best practices within the industry.

Establishing Sterilization Protocols

In the nail salon industry, establishing stringent sterilization protocols is imperative to ensure the safety and well-being of both clients and staff. Effective sterilization protocols involve the meticulous cleaning and disinfection of all reusable instruments and surfaces to prevent the transmission of infections. To commence this process, it is essential to segregate contaminated items from clean ones to thwart any cross-contamination. It is crucial to utilize appropriate personal protective equipment, like gloves and eye protection, when handling contaminated instruments.

The first step in establishing sterilization protocols is to thoroughly clean and scrub all reusable instruments with a suitable detergent and warm water. This initial cleaning procedure is essential for removing visible debris and organic matter from the instruments before they undergo further sterilization processes. After the initial cleaning, the instruments must be submerged in an EPA-approved high-level disinfectant or sterilizing solution. Following manufacturer recommendations is crucial to ensure the effectiveness of the disinfection or sterilization process.

Moreover, implementing a designated area for the sterilization process is integral in organizing and streamlining this critical aspect of salon operations. The sterilization area should be equipped with an autoclave or dry heat sterilizer to effectively sterilize metal instruments. Non-metallic instruments can be disinfected using chemical solutions that have been demonstrated to be effective against pathogens commonly encountered in the salon setting. The sterilization area should be well-ventilated and clearly marked to minimize the risk of cross-contamination.

It is imperative to establish a detailed written protocol outlining each step of the sterilization process, including the frequency of equipment maintenance, testing of sterilization equipment, and employee responsibilities. This protocol should be readily accessible to all staff members and strictly adhered to at all times. Additionally, staff should undergo comprehensive training on proper sterilization techniques and monitoring of sterilization equipment to uphold the highest standards of cleanliness.

Regular auditing and documentation of sterilization processes are vital to validating compliance with established protocols. Monitoring the efficacy of sterilization methods through routine testing and record-keeping reinforces accountability and ensures the consistent application of hygienic practices. By rigorously adhering to these sterilization protocols, nail salons can cultivate a reputation for maintaining uncompromising cleanliness and prioritizing the health and safety of their clientele.

Implementing Waste Disposal Procedures

Proper waste disposal procedures are critical in maintaining a hygienic environment within a nail salon establishment. The handling and management of various types of waste, including biological, chemical, and general refuse, require meticulous attention to detail and strict adherence to regulatory guidelines. This section will delve into the key practices and protocols for implementing effective waste disposal procedures. Firstly, it is essential to categorize waste according to its nature and potential hazards. Biological waste, such as used towels, wipes, and disposable gloves, must be segregated from general waste to prevent cross-contamination. Similarly, chemical waste, including used acetone, nail polish, and disinfectants, should be stored separately to minimize the risk of chemical reactions or leaks. In addition, implementing color-coded waste bins and clearly labeled containers can aid in the proper separation and storage of different waste types. Furthermore, nail salons must establish partnerships with licensed waste management companies to ensure compliant and responsible disposal of hazardous materials. Collaborating with accredited waste collection services guarantees that potentially harmful substances are disposed of safely and in accordance with environmental regulations. Staff training is paramount in enforcing proper waste disposal procedures. Ongoing education on waste segregation, handling, and disposal methods should be provided to all employees. This includes comprehensive guidance on the use of personal protective equipment and spill response protocols to mitigate any potential risks during waste management activities. Additionally, regular audits and assessments of waste disposal procedures should be conducted to identify areas for improvement and ensure consistent compliance. Adhering to best practices for waste disposal not only promotes the health and safety of both salon staff and clients but also demonstrates a commitment to environmental stewardship. By implementing thorough waste disposal procedures, nail salon owners can uphold hygiene standards and contribute to sustainable waste management practices.

Training Staff on Hygiene Best Practices

In the nail salon industry, maintaining high standards of hygiene is paramount to ensure the safety and well-being of both staff and clients. Training staff on hygiene best practices is integral to upholding these standards. Effective training encompasses imparting comprehensive knowledge about sanitation, sterilization, and disinfection protocols. It involves educating employees on the proper use of cleaning agents, personal protective equipment (PPE), and disposal of hazardous materials.

A fundamental aspect of staff training is to instill an understanding of the different types of pathogens and infections that can be spread in a salon environment. This includes educating them on the potential risks associated with improper hygiene practices, such as the transmission of fungal, bacterial, and viral infections. Furthermore, staff should be trained to recognize and address any signs of unsanitary conditions to prevent health hazards.

Training sessions should also cover the identification and proper handling of sterilization equipment and tools. Staff members need to be proficient in utilizing autoclaves, UV sterilizers, and chemical disinfectants according to manufacturer guidelines and industry regulations. They must understand the importance of decontaminating reusable instruments and surfaces between client appointments to minimize the risk of cross-contamination.

Moreover, it is imperative to incorporate practical demonstrations and simulations during the training process. Hands-on exercises provide an opportunity for staff to apply theoretical knowledge into real-world scenarios, thereby reinforcing their understanding and proficiency in executing hygiene best practices. Additionally, incorporating case studies and scenarios about hygiene-related challenges can better prepare them to handle unexpected situations effectively.

Regular assessments and evaluations should be conducted to gauge employees' comprehension and retention of the training material. This feedback-driven approach allows for identifying any areas that may require additional focus or clarification. Moreover, ongoing training and refresher courses should be provided to ensure that staff stay updated on the latest industry standards and best practices.

By prioritizing comprehensive and continuous training on hygiene best practices, nail salon owners can foster a culture of accountability and excellence within their staff, ultimately contributing to a safe and hygienic environment for both employees and clients.

Maintaining Health and Safety Records

Maintaining comprehensive health and safety records is a critical aspect of operating a nail salon business. These records serve as an essential tool for ensuring compliance with hygiene regulations, tracking the implementation of safety measures, and demonstrating a commitment to maintaining a clean and safe environment for both employees and clients.

The first step in maintaining health and safety records involves establishing a systematic recording system. This system should document all aspects related to health and safety, including staff training certifications, equipment maintenance logs, incident reports, and any other relevant documentation. Organizing these records in a well-structured manner allows for easy access and retrieval when needed.

Additionally, it is imperative to regularly update and review these records to reflect any changes or developments in the salon's operations. For example, if new sanitization procedures are introduced or if any health-related incidents occur, these updates should be accurately recorded. Furthermore, conducting periodic audits of the health and safety records ensures that they remain current and reflective of the salon's ongoing commitment to hygiene and safety.

Moreover, maintaining health and safety records is not only about fulfilling regulatory requirements but also about fostering a culture of accountability and transparency within the salon. By documenting the adherence to hygiene protocols and safety guidelines, salon owners and managers demonstrate their dedication to prioritizing the well-being of their staff and clients.

In the event of an inspection or audit by regulatory authorities, comprehensive and organized health and safety records can significantly streamline the process. Inspectors will be able to quickly assess the salon's compliance history, training initiatives, incident management, and overall commitment to maintaining a sanitary and secure environment. This can lead to favorable evaluations and build a positive reputation for the salon within the industry.

Ultimately, maintaining meticulous health and safety records serves as a proactive approach to risk management. It not only minimizes the potential for regulatory fines and penalties but also contributes to fostering trust and confidence among clientele. By upholding high standards of record-keeping related to health and safety, nail salon businesses can uphold their reputation as professional, responsible establishments that prioritize the well-being of their employees and customers.

Conducting Routine Facility Inspections

Effective routine facility inspections are essential in ensuring the ongoing maintenance of health and safety standards within a nail salon. These inspections involve thorough assessments of the physical environment, equipment, and operational processes to identify and address potential hazards and compliance issues. The objective is not only to safeguard the well-being of clients and staff but also to uphold regulatory requirements and industry best practices. A systematic approach to conducting routine facility inspections is vital for sustaining a hygienic and safe operation.

Firstly, it is imperative to establish a comprehensive checklist that outlines all areas requiring inspection, including but not limited to, cleanliness of surfaces, proper storage of products, functionality of ventilation systems, condition of tools, and adherence to sterilization protocols. This checklist should be regularly reviewed and updated to reflect any changes in regulations or internal policies.

Moreover, the frequency of these inspections should be clearly defined, taking into account the size of the salon, foot traffic, and specific risk factors. Whether daily, weekly, or monthly, consistency is key to identifying and addressing concerns in a timely manner. During each inspection, trained staff members or designated safety personnel should thoroughly document their findings, noting any deficiencies or areas for improvement. These records serve as a crucial reference point for tracking the salon's adherence to hygiene and safety standards over time.

Additionally, conducting routine facility inspections offers an opportunity to engage the entire team in prioritizing cleanliness and safety. By involving employees in the inspection process, they develop a deeper understanding of the importance of compliance and are more likely to uphold these standards during their daily responsibilities. This promotes a culture of vigilance and accountability when it comes to maintaining the salon's hygiene.

In summary, conducting routine facility inspections is fundamental to upholding high standards of hygiene, mitigating risks, and demonstrating commitment to regulatory compliance. These inspections not only contribute to the overall professionalism of the salon but also inspire confidence among clientele. By diligently carrying out these inspections, nail salons can continually reinforce their dedication to providing a safe and sanitary environment for both customers and employees.

Adhering to Regulatory Compliance Guidelines

In the nail salon industry, adherence to regulatory compliance guidelines is paramount to ensure the health and safety of both clients and employees. Regulatory bodies such as local health departments, state governing agencies, and federal occupational safety organizations impose stringent regulations to govern various aspects of operations within a nail salon. These regulations encompass a wide range of factors including sanitation, sterilization, ventilation, chemical handling, waste disposal, and more.

One of the fundamental aspects of adhering to regulatory compliance guidelines is understanding the specific requirements set forth by the relevant authorities. This involves thorough research and staying informed about updated regulations and standards in the industry. It also entails maintaining open communication channels with regulatory agencies and seeking clarification when necessary. Nail salon owners and managers must exhibit proactive diligence in interpreting and implementing these guidelines within their establishments.

Moreover, meticulous record-keeping is imperative for demonstrating compliance with regulatory guidelines. Maintaining detailed documentation of sanitation protocols, staff training records, product usage logs, and facility maintenance schedules is essential for audits and inspections. This proactive approach not only ensures legal compliance but also serves as a testament to the salon's commitment to upholding the highest standards of hygiene and safety.

Implementing an effective system for internal auditing and self-assessment is another critical facet of regulatory compliance. This involves conducting regular internal evaluations to identify any deviations from prescribed protocols and promptly addressing any non-compliance issues. It also fosters a culture of continuous improvement and accountability within the salon, further reinforcing its dedication to meeting and exceeding regulatory expectations.

Furthermore, it is essential to integrate regulatory compliance into staff training and onboarding processes. Equipping employees with comprehensive knowledge of regulatory requirements empowers them to uphold these standards in their daily duties. Training should cover proper disinfection techniques, safe handling of chemicals, personal protective equipment usage, and emergency response procedures to ensure that each staff member comprehensively understands and implements regulatory guidelines.

Lastly, staying abreast of emerging technologies, best practices, and industry trends is vital for maintaining compliance with evolving regulations. Regular participation in industry conferences, seminars, and professional development programs can provide valuable insights into advancements in sanitation equipment, procedures, and regulatory updates. By proactively embracing innovation, nail salon owners can adapt their practices to meet the ever-evolving regulatory landscape and position their businesses at the forefront of industry compliance.

In summary, adhering to regulatory compliance guidelines demands unwavering commitment, attention to detail, and a proactive approach to meeting and surpassing established standards. Embracing this responsibility not only safeguards the integrity and reputation of the nail salon but, most importantly, ensures the well-being and confidence of its valued clientele.

Educating Clients on Hygienic Expectations

As a nail salon owner or manager, it is vital to prioritize the health and safety of your clients by educating them on hygienic expectations within the establishment. Firstly, it is imperative to produce informative materials, such as brochures or posters, that outline the salon's commitment to hygiene and the stringent measures in place to ensure a clean and sanitary environment. These materials should be prominently displayed in waiting areas and at service stations, effectively communicating the salon's dedication to upholding exceptional hygiene standards. Moreover, consider utilizing digital platforms, such as the salon's website and social media channels, to disseminate key information on hygienic practices to a wider audience. This includes creating engaging content, such as instructional videos or infographics, to amplify the reach and impact of the educational efforts. Furthermore, during the client intake process, staff should verbally communicate the salon's hygiene protocols and encourage clients to ask any questions they may have. This direct interaction serves to enhance the understanding and appreciation of the comprehensive hygienic measures put in place. Additionally, consider organizing periodic workshops or seminars for both clients and staff, focusing on topics such as infection control, proper hand hygiene, and the importance of using sterilized tools and equipment. These interactive sessions not only reinforce the salon's commitment to hygiene but also empower clients with knowledge that enables them to recognize and demand high standards of cleanliness in any salon setting. Finally, solicit and showcase testimonials from satisfied clients who recognize and appreciate the salon's unwavering dedication to hygiene. By sharing positive experiences and feedback from patrons, the salon can further instill confidence in clients regarding the commitment to upholding stringent hygienic expectations. In conclusion, an informed and educated clientele is crucial in maintaining a culture of rigorous hygiene within a nail salon, and proactive educational initiatives play a pivotal role in achieving this objective.

Responding to Health-Related Incidents

In nail salon establishments, a key aspect of maintaining a safe and hygienic environment is being prepared to respond effectively to health-related incidents. This includes developing protocols and procedures to address various potential issues that may arise in the course of business operations. Responding to health-related incidents encompasses a range of scenarios, from minor injuries to potential outbreaks of infectious diseases.

One crucial aspect of responding to health-related incidents is having well-defined emergency response plans in place. These plans should outline step-by-step procedures for addressing different types of incidents, such as accidents or sudden illness among clients or staff. It is essential for salon owners and managers to ensure that all employees are familiar with these protocols and receive regular training to effectively implement them in real-time situations.

Another vital component of responding to health-related incidents is maintaining communication channels with relevant healthcare authorities and regulatory agencies. Establishing a network of contact persons and understanding reporting requirements for incidents such as suspected infections or safety breaches is critical in ensuring a timely and appropriate response.

Moreover, maintaining thorough documentation related to health-related incidents is imperative. This includes keeping detailed records of any incidents that occur within the salon premises, as well as documenting the actions taken in response. Accurate record-keeping not only enables the salon to track trends and identify areas for improvement but also serves as evidence of compliance with health and safety regulations.

Additionally, in the event of an incident involving a client, it is essential to communicate openly and transparently while respecting their privacy and confidentiality. Salon staff should be trained to handle such situations with empathy and professionalism, providing clear and accurate information while maintaining a supportive atmosphere.

Furthermore, establishing relationships with healthcare professionals and specialists can be beneficial for gaining access to expert advice and guidance when responding to health-related incidents. These connections can provide valuable insights into best practices for handling specific incidents and can contribute to enhancing the overall preparedness of the salon in safeguarding the well-being of both clients and staff.

Finally, conducting regular reviews and assessments of the effectiveness of the response procedures is crucial for continuous improvement. Identifying areas for enhancement and updating protocols based on lessons learned from past incidents ensures that the salon remains proactive and responsive in safeguarding the health and well-being of everyone within its premises.

Quickreads Presents:: Open Your Own Nail Salon

Utilizing Graphs and Grids for Planning

Introduction to Data Visualization

Data visualization is an essential tool for businesses in making informed decisions based on complex sets of data. It involves the graphical representation of information to provide insights, patterns, and trends that may not be immediately evident from raw data. In the context of business planning, data visualization plays a crucial role in identifying opportunities, understanding market trends, and assessing the effectiveness of strategies. The use of visual elements such as graphs, charts, and grids facilitates the communication of quantitative data, enabling stakeholders to comprehend and interpret information more effectively. With the increasing volume of data generated by businesses, the ability to visualize and understand this data is becoming paramount in driving strategic decision-making. Data visualization not only simplifies complex data but also presents it in a format that is easily digestible and actionable. This section will delve into the significance of data visualization in business planning and provide insights into the various techniques and tools employed for effective visualization. By gaining a thorough understanding of data visualization, businesses can harness the power of visual representation to drive growth, innovation, and competitive advantage.

Types of Graphs and Grids for Business Planning

In the realm of business planning, the effective representation of data through graphs and grids plays a pivotal role in facilitating informed decision-making. Various types of graphs and grids are employed to visually communicate complex information and trends. One of the most commonly used graphs is the line graph, which is instrumental in illustrating trends over time. This type of graph is valuable for displaying changes in key performance indicators or market trends. Another essential graph is the bar chart, which is adept at comparing categorical data across different groups or time periods. A pie chart, while often criticized for its limited use, can effectively depict parts of a whole concept, making it useful for showcasing percentages and proportions in business planning. Moving to more specialized forms of graphical representation, scatter plots are employed to illustrate the relationship between two variables, aiding in identifying patterns or outliers within the data. Furthermore, histograms provide a visual representation of the distribution of numerical data, indicating frequency and patterns within a dataset. Utilizing specialized grids, such as heatmaps, allows for the visual interpretation of data clusters and trends. Heatmaps enable executives to identify both strengths and vulnerabilities within their business operations. Additionally, the implementation of dashboards incorporating various graphs and grids enables real-time monitoring of key metrics, providing a comprehensive overview of the business landscape. As businesses continue to grow more data-driven, the ability to harness the power of these graphical representations becomes increasingly imperative for effective strategic planning and informed decision-making.

Data Collection and Analysis Techniques

Data collection and analysis techniques are foundational to effective business planning. In the nail salon industry, gathering and interpreting relevant data is crucial for making informed decisions. The process starts with identifying key performance indicators (KPIs) such as customer footfall, service utilization rates, product sales, and operational expenses. Once the KPIs are identified, it is essential to establish streamlined data collection methods. This can include implementing customer management systems, point-of-sale software, and employee performance tracking tools. Additionally, surveys and feedback mechanisms can provide valuable qualitative data for analysis.

The next step involves data analysis techniques to derive meaningful insights. This includes leveraging statistical methods to identify trends, correlations, and outliers within the collected data. Various analytical tools can be employed such as regression analysis, time series analysis, and cohort analysis to uncover patterns and relationships. Furthermore, employing data visualization techniques through graphs, charts, and dashboards can aid in presenting complex data in a comprehensible manner.

Moreover, utilizing Excel for data analysis allows for robust manipulation and interpretation of large datasets. Functions such as pivot tables, data filtering, and conditional formatting enable stakeholders to dissect and scrutinize data from different angles. When dealing with customer-related data, segmentation and RFM (Recency, Frequency, Monetary) analysis can further refine the understanding of customer behavior and preferences.

It's imperative to ensure the accuracy and integrity of the collected data through rigorous validation processes. This involves cross-referencing data points, applying outlier detection algorithms, and implementing data cleaning methodologies to mitigate errors and discrepancies. Embracing data governance frameworks and best practices also plays a pivotal role in maintaining data quality and consistency.

In conclusion, mastering data collection and analysis techniques empowers nail salon entrepreneurs to make data-driven decisions that positively impact their business. By meticulously gathering, analyzing, and validating data, salon owners and managers can gain a deeper understanding of their operations, customer behavior, and market dynamics, ultimately leading to strategic and sustainable business planning.

Utilizing Excel for Graphical Representation

In the realm of business planning and decision-making, graphical representation plays a pivotal role in transforming raw data into actionable insights. One of the most widely used and versatile tools for graphical representation is Microsoft Excel. Leveraging Excel's array of features, from basic graphs to advanced visualization techniques, empowers entrepreneurs to make informed decisions based on comprehensive data analysis. Excel offers a diverse range of chart types such as line graphs, bar charts, pie charts, and scatter plots, each serving unique purposes in visualizing different types of business data. Furthermore, Excel facilitates the creation of complex graphs, providing users with customizable options to tailor visualizations according to specific business requirements. For instance, through Excel's pivot charts, entrepreneurs can dynamically organize and display vast datasets, helping identify trends and patterns essential for strategic planning. Additionally, Excel integrates seamlessly with other analytical tools, bolstering its capability to handle large volumes of data and render graphical representation with exceptional precision. Moreover, by utilizing Excel's built-in functions and formulas, entrepreneurs can automate data visualization processes, ensuring consistency and accuracy in graphical representation. Equally significant is the ability to link Excel charts to real-time data sources, enabling the creation of dynamic dashboards that update automatically as new data is inputted. This feature not only enhances the relevance of graphical representation but also streamlines the decision-making process. In conclusion, leveraging Excel for graphical representation equips entrepreneurs with the means to transform intricate datasets into visually appealing and informative representations, providing a solid foundation for informed business decisions.

Implementing Dashboard Metrics

In the nail salon industry, where success hinges on meticulous planning and strategic decision-making, implementing dashboard metrics is imperative for monitoring the performance of various business aspects. Dashboard metrics serve as a visual representation of key performance indicators (KPIs) and provide immediate insights into the health of the business. Dashboards offer a real-time snapshot of critical data, aiding in identifying trends, detecting anomalies, and facilitating timely interventions. This section will delve into the intricate process of designing and implementing effective dashboard metrics tailored to the specific requirements of a nail salon business.

Selecting the appropriate KPIs is the foundation of effective dashboard metrics. These KPIs must align with the overarching business objectives and reflect the unique dynamics of the nail salon industry. Common KPIs in this context may include customer retention rates, average revenue per customer, service utilization levels, inventory turnover ratios, and employee productivity metrics. Each selected KPI must be quantifiable, relevant, and actionable to ensure meaningful interpretation and informed decision-making.

Once the KPIs are defined, the next step involves choosing the most suitable data visualization techniques for dashboard representation. Graphs, charts, and other visual elements should be meticulously chosen to effectively communicate the underlying trends and patterns inherent in the data. Utilizing line graphs for showcasing trends over time, pie charts for illustrating proportional distribution, and bar graphs for performance comparisons can offer valuable insights into the operational efficiency and financial viability of the nail salon establishment.

Additionally, the design and layout of the dashboard deserve careful consideration. Clarity, simplicity, and intuitive arrangement are pivotal to ensuring that users can swiftly comprehend the displayed metrics. The use of color coding, customized widgets, and interactive elements can enhance user engagement and facilitate swift identification of critical information. Furthermore, incorporating drill-down capabilities can empower stakeholders to delve deeper into specific metrics, enabling comprehensive analysis and targeted interventions.

Moreover, dashboard metrics should not be static; they must evolve in response to shifting business dynamics and emerging trends. Implementing dynamic dashboards that automatically update with real-time data feeds can enable proactive decision-making and ensure that the metrics remain relevant and reflective of the current business landscape.

In conclusion, by effectively implementing dashboard metrics encompassing carefully selected KPIs, judicious data visualization techniques, and user-centric design principles, nail salon owners and managers can harness the power of actionable insights to steer their businesses towards sustained growth and profitability.

Utilizing Heatmaps for Trend Analysis

Heatmaps are effective visual tools for analyzing trends and patterns within large datasets. In the context of nail salon business planning, heatmaps can be utilized to examine various aspects such as customer attendance patterns, product sales trends, and even employee productivity over specific time periods. The use of color gradients in heatmaps allows for the quick identification of high and low activity areas, providing valuable insights into the dynamics of the nail salon business. Understanding the utilization of heatmaps involves proper data preprocessing and selection of relevant variables for analysis. It is crucial to ensure that the data being visualized is accurately represented without any bias or errors. Once the data is prepared, heatmap generation tools such as Python's seaborn library or Tableau can be employed for creating visually engaging representations. These heatmaps can then be used to identify peak hours for appointments, popular nail art designs, or fluctuations in customer preferences. Furthermore, heatmaps allow for the identification of correlations between different factors, aiding in informed decision-making for resource allocation and strategic planning. Interpretation of heatmaps requires an understanding of scale and color mapping, ensuring that the portrayed trends are easily comprehensible to stakeholders. Moreover, the ability to differentiate between meaningful patterns and random noise within the heatmaps is essential for drawing accurate conclusions. By leveraging heatmaps for trend analysis, nail salon owners and managers can gain actionable insights to optimize operations, enhance customer experiences, and drive business growth.

Interpreting Correlation Coefficients

In the realm of data analysis, interpreting correlation coefficients plays a vital role in understanding the relationships between variables. Correlation coefficients measure the strength and direction of a linear relationship between two variables. This statistical concept aids business owners and decision-makers in making informed choices based on empirical evidence.

The coefficient values range from -1 to 1, indicating the strength and direction of the relationship. A value of 1 suggests a perfect positive linear relationship, while -1 indicates a perfect negative linear relationship. A value of 0 suggests no linear relationship between the variables.

Interpreting correlation coefficients involves assessing the magnitude of the value. A coefficient close to 1 or -1 signifies a strong linear relationship, whereas a coefficient near 0 implies a weak or non-existent relationship. Additionally, the sign of the coefficient indicates the direction of the relationship - positive, negative, or neutral.

Further scrutiny of correlation coefficients should consider the significance level of the correlation, often denoted by a p-value. A low p-value suggests that the observed correlation is unlikely to be due to random chance, reinforcing the validity of the relationship.

When evaluating correlation coefficients, it is essential to remember that correlation does not imply causation. While a significant correlation coefficient may highlight a strong association between variables, it does not establish a cause-and-effect relationship. Cautious consideration and additional contextual information are paramount to drawing accurate conclusions.

Correlation coefficients find widespread application in various business contexts, such as market research, financial analysis, and operational decision-making. Understanding and correctly interpreting these coefficients empower entrepreneurs and executives to harness the power of quantitative data for strategic planning, risk assessment, and performance optimization.

In conclusion, interpreting correlation coefficients demands a meticulous approach, encompassing the magnitude, direction, and significance level of the coefficient. Embracing this analytical tool equips stakeholders with valuable insights, enabling them to make well-informed decisions grounded in empirical evidence and statistical rigor.

Optimizing Graphical Representations for Decision Making

In the modern business landscape, making informed decisions is crucial for the success of any enterprise. To facilitate this process, the utilization of graphical representations has become an integral part of strategic decision-making. Optimizing graphical representations involves employing a range of visualization techniques to effectively communicate complex data and insights. This section explores the pivotal role of optimized graphical representations in enhancing decision-making processes within the nail salon industry.

When it comes to optimizing graphical representations for decision making, one must first consider the choice of graphs and charts. Selecting the most appropriate visual representation is paramount as it directly impacts the clarity and understanding of the presented data. Bar charts, line graphs, pie charts, and scatter plots are commonly used to represent different types of data. Understanding which type of graph best suits the dataset at hand is essential for accurately conveying the information to stakeholders and decision-makers. Moreover, the effective use of color, scale, and labeling within these graphical representations can significantly enhance their interpretability and impact.

Another crucial aspect of optimization is the integration of data analytics into graphical representations. Advanced analytics techniques can be leveraged to extract meaningful insights from large datasets, allowing for more informed decisions. By integrating statistical measures and trend analysis into graphical representations, decision-makers gain access to valuable, actionable intelligence that can drive strategic initiatives within the nail salon industry. Additionally, the integration of interactive features within graphical representations, such as zoom functions and filter options, provides decision-makers with the ability to delve deeper into the data, thus facilitating a more thorough understanding of the underlying trends and patterns.

Furthermore, the use of dashboard metrics plays a pivotal role in optimizing graphical representations for decision making. Dashboards offer a comprehensive overview of key performance indicators (KPIs) and critical metrics, enabling decision-makers to monitor the health and progress of various aspects of the nail salon business. Through visually appealing and intuitive dashboards, managers and stakeholders can quickly assimilate vital information, identify trends, and make timely, well-informed decisions. The dynamic nature of dashboard metrics allows for real-time tracking of performance, thereby empowering decision-makers to react promptly to changes in the business environment.

Overall, the optimization of graphical representations for decision making represents an indispensable aspect of strategic management within the nail salon industry. By harnessing the power of advanced visualization techniques, data analytics, and interactive dashboards, stakeholders and decision-makers can gain deeper insights, derive meaningful conclusions, and drive the business forward with confidence and precision.

Implementing Gantt Charts for Project Management

In the realm of project management, the implementation of Gantt charts has proven to be an invaluable tool for planning, coordinating, and tracking project tasks. Named after Henry Gantt, who designed them in the 1910s, Gantt charts provide a visual representation of a project schedule that allows project managers and teams to comprehensively view the various tasks, their dependencies, timelines, and progress. This section will delve into the intricacies of implementing Gantt charts and their significance in orchestrating successful project management.

One of the primary advantages of using Gantt charts is their ability to display the sequence of project activities and their respective durations. This sequential visualization enables project managers to effectively allocate resources, identify potential bottlenecks, and optimize the project timeline. Furthermore, Gantt charts facilitate the identification of task dependencies, allowing for the clear understanding of which tasks must be completed before others can commence.

Moreover, Gantt charts play a pivotal role in communication and collaboration within project teams. By presenting a visual project timeline with clear milestones and deadlines, team members can have a comprehensive overview of the project's progression and their individual responsibilities. This transparency fosters accountability, encourages proactive problem-solving, and empowers team members to manage their time and tasks efficiently.

With the advent of digital project management tools and software, Gantt charts have become more dynamic and interactive, offering real-time updates, resource allocation features, and the integration of dependencies and constraints. These advancements elevate the utility and accessibility of Gantt charts, enabling project managers to adapt and modify project schedules swiftly in response to changing circumstances or priorities.

As organizations embrace agile methodologies and adaptive project management approaches, Gantt charts continue to evolve to accommodate iterative and incremental project lifecycles. Their adaptability makes them compatible with diverse project management frameworks, providing a visual roadmap for project teams to navigate through complex initiatives while maintaining clarity on deadlines, deliverables, and critical path analysis.

In summary, the implementation of Gantt charts for project management facilitates efficient resource allocation, transparent communication, proactive problem-solving, and adaptability to evolving project dynamics. As organizations strive for heightened efficiency and effectiveness in project execution, leveraging Gantt charts as a core component of project management processes remains integral to achieving successful outcomes.

Leveraging Quantitative Analysis for Strategic Planning

In the context of nail salon business, leveraging quantitative analysis for strategic planning is imperative for long-term success and sustainability. Quantitative analysis involves the use of data and statistical models to gain valuable insights and make informed decisions. When applied to strategic planning, it enables salon owners to assess various factors influencing the business, identify trends, and forecast future performance. This section will explore how nail salon entrepreneurs can effectively leverage quantitative analysis for strategic planning.

Strategic planning in the nail salon industry requires a meticulous approach towards understanding customer preferences, market trends, and operational efficiency. Quantitative analysis offers a structured methodology to examine key performance indicators (KPIs) such as customer retention rates, average service utilization per client, and revenue per service category. By collecting and analyzing this data, salon owners can gain a comprehensive understanding of their business's performance.

Furthermore, quantitative analysis facilitates the identification of growth opportunities and potential threats. Through the use of statistical tools and techniques, such as regression analysis and forecasting models, salon owners can predict demand patterns, seasonality effects, and competitive dynamics within the market. This proactive approach enables them to make data-driven decisions regarding resource allocation, pricing strategies, and marketing initiatives.

Moreover, leveraging quantitative analysis allows nail salon entrepreneurs to optimize their resource utilization and operational efficiency. By employing statistical process control and performance benchmarking, salon owners can identify areas for improvement in service delivery, inventory management, and staffing. This data-driven approach empowers them to streamline operations, reduce costs, and enhance overall customer satisfaction.

Additionally, quantitative analysis plays a pivotal role in risk management and scenario planning for nail salons. Through statistical risk modeling and sensitivity analysis, salon owners can assess the potential impact of external factors such as economic downturns, regulatory changes, or supply chain disruptions. This foresight enables them to develop contingency plans and strategic responses, ensuring resilience in the face of unforeseen challenges.

In conclusion, leveraging quantitative analysis for strategic planning empowers nail salon entrepreneurs to make informed, data-driven decisions that are crucial for long-term success. By harnessing the power of data and statistical insights, salon owners can gain a competitive edge, adapt to market dynamics, and drive sustainable growth in the nail salon business.

Quickreads Presents:: Open Your Own Nail Salon

Crafting Effective Marketing Strategies

Analyzing Target Market

To effectively craft marketing strategies, it is imperative to thoroughly analyze the target market. This involves a multifaceted approach that utilizes both quantitative and qualitative data. Quantitative data includes demographic information, such as age, gender, income level, and location, which provides insights into the specific segments of the market. Additionally, behavioral data, like purchase history and frequency of salon visits, helps in understanding consumer patterns and preferences. Qualitative data, on the other hand, involves gaining an in-depth understanding of customers' motivations, needs, and aspirations through surveys, interviews, and focus groups. It's essential to combine these data sets to develop comprehensive buyer personas that represent the typical characteristics and behaviors of the target audience.

Furthermore, analyzing the competition within the nail salon industry is crucial. By conducting a competitive analysis, we can identify the strengths, weaknesses, opportunities, and threats posed by existing nail salons. This involves examining factors such as pricing strategies, service offerings, promotional tactics, and customer satisfaction levels. Understanding how competitors position themselves in the market and how they are perceived by consumers enables us to differentiate our own salon effectively. Moreover, scanning industry trends and forecasts provides valuable insights into evolving consumer preferences and market dynamics. This allows for the identification of emerging opportunities and potential threats that could impact the salon's market positioning.

Conducting a thorough market analysis also involves utilizing tools and techniques such as SWOT analysis, PESTEL analysis, and Porter's Five Forces framework. These methodologies enable a structured evaluation of the internal and external factors influencing the target market, including assessing the salon's internal capabilities, economic and political trends, technological advancements, social and cultural influences, as well as the bargaining power of suppliers and buyers. By delving deep into these analytical frameworks, we gain a holistic understanding of the market landscape and are better equipped to make informed decisions regarding the formulation of marketing strategies that resonate with the identified target audience.

Utilizing Data-Driven Approaches

Utilizing data-driven approaches is paramount in today's competitive business landscape, particularly within the nail salon industry. By harnessing the power of data, salon owners and marketers can gain valuable insights into consumer behavior, preferences, and trends, enabling them to make informed decisions and optimize their marketing strategies. Data-driven approaches involve the collection, analysis, and interpretation of various types of data, including customer demographics, purchasing patterns, online behavior, and market trends. With the proliferation of digital tools and platforms, businesses can access an abundance of data sources, ranging from website analytics and social media metrics to customer relationship management (CRM) systems and industry reports. One of the primary benefits of data-driven approaches is the ability to segment and target specific audience groups more effectively. Through data analysis, nail salon businesses can identify niche markets, understand the needs and interests of different customer segments, and tailor their marketing messages and promotions accordingly. Additionally, data-driven approaches facilitate the measurement of marketing campaign performance. By tracking key performance indicators (KPIs) such as conversion rates, customer acquisition costs, and engagement metrics, salon owners can assess the effectiveness of their marketing efforts and make data-backed adjustments to optimize their return on investment. Moreover, data-driven approaches enable the personalization of marketing initiatives. Armed with insights from customer data, salon businesses can create personalized experiences for their clients, offering targeted promotions, customized services, and relevant content that resonates with individual preferences. This level of personalization not only enhances customer satisfaction but also fosters long-term loyalty and strengthens brand affinity. Another crucial aspect of utilizing data-driven approaches is the continual refinement of marketing strategies. By regularly monitoring and analyzing data, salon owners can identify emerging trends, shifting consumer behaviors, and evolving market dynamics. This proactive approach allows businesses to adapt quickly, innovate their marketing tactics, and stay ahead of the competition. Ultimately, embracing data-driven approaches empowers nail salon businesses to make strategic, well-informed marketing decisions, maximize their reach and impact, and achieve sustainable growth in a rapidly evolving industry.

Implementing Search Engine Optimization (SEO) Tactics

Search Engine Optimization (SEO) tactics are crucial for enhancing the online presence of a nail salon business. By strategically incorporating SEO practices, businesses can improve their website's visibility and attract potential customers. A comprehensive approach to SEO involves several key tactics. Firstly, conducting thorough keyword research to identify relevant search terms that potential customers may use when seeking nail salon services.

Implementing these keywords naturally within website content, meta tags, and headlines can significantly boost search engine rankings. Additionally, optimizing website loading speed, mobile responsiveness, and user experience contributes to higher search engine rankings. Furthermore, creating high-quality, relevant content and obtaining backlinks from reputable websites are integral components of an effective SEO strategy. It is essential to stay updated with the latest search engine algorithms and trends to adapt the SEO approach accordingly, ensuring sustained visibility and traffic. It's also vital to conduct regular performance analysis using tools such as Google Analytics to monitor the impact of SEO efforts and make data-driven adjustments. Ultimately, by mastering SEO tactics, nail salon businesses can increase their online visibility, attract more organic traffic, and outperform competitors in the digital landscape.

Leveraging Social Media Platforms

In the digital age, social media has emerged as a pivotal avenue for nail salon businesses to engage with their target audience, build brand awareness, and drive customer acquisition. Leveraging social media platforms involves a strategic approach that encompasses various elements of content, engagement, and data analysis. Firstly, it is imperative to identify the most suitable social media channels for the nail salon industry, considering factors such as visual appeal and audience demographics. Once identified, an in-depth understanding of each platform's algorithms and best practices is essential to maximize organic reach and engagement. Utilizing visual content, such as high-quality images and videos showcasing nail artistry, can captivate the audience and stimulate interest in the salon's services. Additionally, maintaining a consistent posting schedule and utilizing relevant hashtags can amplify the salon's visibility and reach a wider audience. Engaging with followers through interactive posts, stories, and live sessions fosters a sense of community and strengthens brand loyalty. Moreover, monitoring social media insights and metrics is crucial for refining strategies and understanding audience behavior. Analyzing key performance indicators (KPIs) such as engagement rate, click-through rate, and conversion rate provides valuable insights for optimizing social media campaigns. Furthermore, leveraging social media advertising platforms allows for targeted promotions and retargeting strategies to effectively reach potential customers. Collaborating with influencers in the beauty and lifestyle niche can significantly expand the salon's reach and tap into new customer segments. Building a cohesive social media strategy that aligns with the nail salon's brand identity and values is paramount for establishing a strong online presence and fostering meaningful connections with the audience. By harnessing the full potential of social media platforms, nail salon businesses can cultivate a thriving digital community and drive sustainable growth.

Creating Compelling Content Strategy

In the digital landscape of the nail salon industry, creating a compelling content strategy is paramount to engage and retain customers. This strategy encompasses the creation, curation, and distribution of various types of content across multiple platforms to resonate with the target audience and drive brand awareness. The goal is to position the nail salon as a knowledgeable and trustworthy authority in the industry, ultimately converting leads into loyal customers.

First and foremost, identifying the target audience is crucial in tailoring the content strategy. Whether it's informative blogs, visually appealing images, or engaging videos, the content should address the pain points, desires, and interests of the potential clientele. Additionally, the content must align with the brand identity and reflect the unique selling propositions of the nail salon.

Moreover, leveraging Search Engine Optimization (SEO) practices within the content becomes imperative for improved visibility. This involves researching relevant keywords, optimizing meta descriptions, and crafting compelling headlines to enhance the discoverability of the content on search engines, thus driving organic traffic to the salon's digital platforms.

Furthermore, an effective content strategy integrates a mix of educational, entertaining, and promotional content to maintain a balanced approach. Educational content serves to inform the audience about nail care tips, latest trends, and salon procedures, positioning the salon as an industry expert. Entertainment-focused content aims to engage the audience through behind-the-scenes glimpses, customer testimonials, and engaging visuals to foster a sense of community and inclusivity. Lastly, promotional content subtly promotes the salon's products, services, and special offers, intertwining them seamlessly with valuable information.

The frequency and consistency of content publication are also vital considerations. A well-defined editorial calendar ensures a steady stream of content, keeping the audience engaged and fostering long-term relationships. Furthermore, tracking and analyzing the performance of each piece of content using analytics tools enable continuous optimization of the strategy based on audience preferences and engagement metrics.

In conclusion, with the increasing reliance on digital platforms for information and entertainment, a compelling content strategy plays a pivotal role in differentiating a nail salon from competitors, establishing its online presence, and nurturing customer trust and loyalty.

Building Email Marketing Campaigns

Building an effective email marketing campaign is a crucial component of a comprehensive marketing strategy for a nail salon business. With the potential to reach a targeted audience directly in their inbox, email campaigns can drive customer engagement, retention, and ultimately, revenue. To construct successful email marketing campaigns, it is essential to focus on several key elements. Firstly, segmentation of the email list is paramount. By categorizing subscribers based on their preferences, behaviors, and demographics, personalized and relevant content can be delivered, resulting in higher open and click-through rates. Additionally, the design and layout of the emails should be visually appealing, mobile-responsive, and aligned with the brand's aesthetic to ensure a positive user experience. Moreover, crafting compelling subject lines and concise yet impactful copy is vital to capture recipients' attention and prompt action. A/B testing different elements such as subject lines, visuals, and call-to-action buttons can provide valuable insights into audience preferences and optimize campaign performance. Furthermore, leveraging automation tools to schedule and send targeted emails based on subscriber actions, such as welcome sequences, birthday offers, or abandoned cart reminders, can enhance customer engagement and drive conversions. It is equally important to measure the success of email campaigns through key performance indicators (KPIs) such as open rates, click-through rates, conversion rates, and unsubscribe rates. Regular analysis of these metrics enables continuous refinement and improvement of email marketing strategies. Additionally, complying with data protection regulations and privacy best practices is imperative to maintain trust and transparency with subscribers. By adhering to industry standards and obtaining explicit consent for sending promotional emails, businesses can safeguard their reputation and build long-term relationships with customers. In conclusion, building impactful email marketing campaigns involves meticulous planning, personalized content creation, strategic deployment, continual optimization, and ethical compliance. When executed effectively, email campaigns can serve as a powerful tool to nurture customer loyalty, drive traffic to the salon, and boost overall business growth.

Understanding Key Performance Indicators (KPIs)

Key Performance Indicators (KPIs) are critical metrics used to evaluate the success of a nail salon's marketing efforts and overall business performance. By understanding and effectively utilizing KPIs, owners and managers can make informed decisions to drive growth and maximize profitability. There are various KPIs that are particularly relevant to the nail salon industry. One of the primary KPIs is customer acquisition cost (CAC), which measures the cost of acquiring new customers through marketing and advertising efforts. This metric helps in determining the effectiveness of marketing strategies and allows for adjustments to optimize ROI. Additionally, customer retention rate is a crucial KPI that reflects the salon's ability to maintain a loyal client base. Monitoring this metric enables the identification of trends and patterns, leading to improved client retention strategies. Another essential KPI is the average revenue per customer visit, which provides insights into the salon's sales performance and the value generated from each customer. Tracking this KPI helps in tailoring promotions and upselling techniques to increase the average spend per visit. Furthermore, the conversion rate from initial inquiry to actual appointment booking is a key indicator of the effectiveness of the salon's customer service and sales processes. Understanding the factors influencing this conversion rate allows for targeted improvements in service delivery and customer experience. Moreover, social media engagement metrics, such as likes, shares, and comments, play a significant role in evaluating the impact of the salon's online presence and content strategy. Analyzing these metrics aids in refining social media campaigns and enhancing brand visibility. As technology continues to evolve, digital KPIs like website traffic, click-through rates, and online appointment bookings have become indispensable measures for evaluating the effectiveness of a salon's online marketing initiatives. Implementing robust analytical tools and systems to track and interpret these KPIs is essential for making data-driven marketing decisions. In conclusion, understanding and leveraging KPIs is fundamental for driving the success of a nail salon, empowering stakeholders to continuously improve and refine their marketing strategies and operational methodologies.

Implementing A/B Testing for Campaigns

A/B testing, also known as split testing, is a vital component of any comprehensive marketing strategy in the nail salon industry. By systematically comparing two versions of a marketing asset, such as an advertisement or a landing page, businesses can gather valuable insights into consumer behavior and preferences. This quantitative approach enables data-driven decision-making, optimizing campaign performance to maximize conversion rates and return on investment.

To begin implementing A/B testing for campaigns, it is crucial to first define clear and measurable objectives. Whether the goal is to increase appointment bookings, promote a new service, or drive product sales, establishing specific key performance indicators (KPIs) is essential. These KPIs may include click-through rates, bounce rates, or form submissions, depending on the nature of the campaign.

Once the objectives and KPIs are defined, the next step is to identify the elements to be tested. Common variables for A/B testing in nail salon marketing campaigns may include call-to-action buttons, ad copy, imagery, color schemes, and promotional offers. Each element should be selected based on its potential impact on the target audience's decision-making process.

After identifying the testing elements, a robust testing methodology must be devised. This involves creating two distinct versions of the marketing asset, ensuring that only one variable is altered between the versions. It is imperative to maintain consistency in other aspects to accurately measure the isolated impact of the tested element.

Subsequently, an appropriate A/B testing tool or platform should be chosen to execute the experiment. Various digital marketing tools offer built-in A/B testing capabilities, allowing for seamless deployment and accurate tracking of campaign variations. Additionally, these platforms often provide statistical significance calculations to determine the validity of the test results.

Once the A/B testing is live, meticulous data collection and analysis are imperative. Accurate tracking of user interactions and conversions is essential to draw meaningful conclusions from the experiment. Statistical methods such as hypothesis testing and confidence intervals can be employed to interpret the results and ascertain the effectiveness of the tested elements.

Based on the insights derived from A/B testing, iterative refinements can be made to nail salon marketing campaigns, continually enhancing their efficacy and resonance with the target audience. Furthermore, the knowledge gained from successful A/B tests can inform future marketing strategies, fostering a culture of continuous improvement and innovation within the nail salon business.

Engaging in Influencer Partnerships

In today's digital landscape, influencer partnerships have become an integral part of marketing strategies for businesses across various industries. Engaging with influencers allows nail salon businesses to tap into a wider audience and leverage the existing follower base of these influential individuals. A successful influencer partnership can significantly amplify brand exposure, drive engagement, and ultimately lead to an increase in customer acquisition. When selecting influencers to partner with, it is essential to consider relevance to the nail salon industry. Identifying influencers whose content aligns with the brand's image and values is crucial for establishing authentic connections with the target audience. Additionally, assessing an influencer's reach, engagement rate, and audience demographics is vital for determining the potential impact of the partnership. Once suitable influencers are identified, establishing clear partnership terms and objectives is paramount. This includes outlining deliverables, such as sponsored posts, reviews, or event appearances, as well as specifying key performance indicators (KPIs) to measure the success of the collaboration. Effective communication and transparency in expectations form the foundation of a fruitful influencer partnership. Furthermore, fostering genuine relationships with influencers beyond transactional arrangements can lead to long-term collaborations and advocacy for the nail salon brand. Leveraging influencer-generated content across various marketing channels can enhance the overall brand narrative and resonate with the target demographic. However, it is crucial for businesses to comply with relevant advertising regulations and ensure that influencer content is transparently labeled as sponsored or paid, maintaining ethical practices. Continuously evaluating the performance of influencer partnerships through metrics such as engagement rates, referral traffic, and conversion data enables businesses to refine their approach and optimize future collaborations. In conclusion, engaging in influencer partnerships presents a valuable opportunity for nail salon businesses to expand their reach, build credibility, and foster meaningful connections with consumers in an increasingly competitive market.

Measuring Return on Investment (ROI)

Measuring the return on investment (ROI) is a critical aspect of assessing the effectiveness of marketing strategies in the nail salon industry. ROI quantifies the financial benefit obtained from a particular investment relative to the cost of that investment. In the context of influencer partnerships, accurately measuring ROI can provide valuable insights into the impact of these collaborations on the overall business performance. The calculation of ROI involves comparing the net gain from the investment with the initial cost of the investment.

To calculate the ROI of influencer partnerships, nail salon owners can track various metrics such as increased foot traffic, online engagement, and direct sales linked to influencer promotions. Moreover, it is essential to consider the qualitative benefits brought by influencer partnerships, including brand visibility, social media mentions, and brand sentiment.

When evaluating ROI, it's imperative to distinguish between the immediate and long-term effects of influencer partnerships. This entails analyzing customer retention rates, lifetime value of acquired customers, and brand loyalty stemming from influencer endorsements. Integrating data analytics tools, such as customer relationship management (CRM) systems and social listening platforms, enables a comprehensive assessment of the impact of influencer partnerships on ROI.

Furthermore, implementing attribution models that attribute conversions to specific marketing touchpoints can refine the ROI measurement process. By employing multi-touch attribution models, nail salon businesses can understand the contribution of influencer content across various stages of the customer journey, subsequently refining ROI calculations.

In addition to quantitative measurements, qualitative assessments play a pivotal role in evaluating the ROI of influencer partnerships. Surveys, focus groups, and sentiment analysis can provide nuanced insights into consumer perceptions influenced by influencer collaborations, enriching the understanding of ROI beyond monetary metrics.

To optimize ROI measurement, establishing clear KPIs aligned with the objectives of influencer partnerships is crucial. Whether the goal is to increase brand awareness, drive foot traffic, or boost product sales, aligning KPIs with specific outcomes facilitates precise ROI evaluation.

In conclusion, measuring the ROI of influencer partnerships in the nail salon industry demands a comprehensive approach encompassing both quantitative and qualitative assessments. By leveraging an array of metrics, data analytics tools, and clear KPIs, nail salon owners can effectively gauge the impact of influencer collaborations on business performance and make data-driven decisions for future marketing strategies.

Quickreads Presents:: Open Your Own Nail Salon

Managing Customer Relations

Value-Added Services for Elevated Customer Relations: Offering value-added services can significantly contribute to building strong customer relations in the salon industry. Beyond the core nail care services, salons can provide complimentary amenities such as hand massages, refreshments, or personalized consultations to elevate the overall client experience. These additional services not only demonstrate the salon's commitment to client well-being but also create opportunities for meaningful interactions that foster rapport and trust.

Creating a Personalized Loyalty Program: A well-crafted loyalty program tailored to clients' preferences and spending behaviors can incentivize repeat business and strengthen customer relations. By offering personalized rewards, exclusive perks, and tiered benefits based on client engagement, salons can instill a sense of appreciation and value, encouraging long-term loyalty and advocacy among their clients.

Tailoring the Physical Environment for Client Comfort: The physical ambiance of a salon plays a significant role in shaping the client experience. Attention to detail in creating a comfortable and inviting atmosphere, from soothing decor to comfortable seating and ambient music, can contribute to a positive and memorable client experience. By curating an environment that aligns with clients' preferences and promotes relaxation, salons can create a welcoming space that enhances customer relations.

Empathetic Conflict Resolution and Service Recovery: In moments of service issues or customer dissatisfaction, the way a salon handles the situation can profoundly impact customer relations. Training staff to approach conflicts with empathy, active listening, and a proactive service recovery mindset can turn a negative experience into an opportunity to strengthen client relations. By promptly addressing concerns and demonstrating genuine care for the client's well-being, salons can mitigate potential grievances and reinforce their commitment to client satisfaction.

Personal Connections Through Client Recognition: Personalized client recognition can go a long way in building strong customer relations. Simple gestures such as addressing clients by name, remembering their preferences, or asking about important milestones in their lives can make clients feel valued and appreciated. These personal connections foster a sense of belonging and loyalty, creating an emotional bond that extends beyond the transactional aspect of salon visits.

Leveraging Social Media for Engagement and Customer Relations: Social media platforms offer valuable opportunities for salons to engage with clients and build customer relations outside of the salon environment. By sharing behind-the-scenes content, client testimonials, and interactive polls, salons can foster a sense of community, encourage dialogue, and showcase their commitment to customer satisfaction. Additionally, actively responding to client inquiries and feedback on social media platforms demonstrates accessibility and responsiveness, contributing to a positive client experience.

Personal Development and Relationship-Building for Staff: Investing in the personal development and relationship-building skills of salon staff can have a profound impact on customer relations. By providing training in emotional intelligence, effective communication, and relationship-building techniques, salons can empower their employees to cultivate genuine connections with clients and deliver exceptional customer experiences that resonate on a personal level.

Proactive Client Education on Nail Health and Care: Beyond providing nail care services, salons can proactively educate clients on nail health and care best practices. By sharing insights on nail maintenance, hygiene protocols, and product recommendations, salons can position themselves as trusted advisors focused on the overall well-being of their clients. This educational approach not only fortifies trust but also empowers clients to make informed decisions about their nail care, strengthening the salon-client relationship.

Personal Client Appreciation Notes and Gestures: Cultivating strong customer relations can be as simple as offering personalized notes of appreciation or small gestures of gratitude. Handwritten thank-you notes, birthday cards, or small tokens of appreciation can demonstrate thoughtfulness and care, leaving a lasting impression on clients and reinforcing the salon's commitment to building meaningful relationships beyond the standard service interactions.

Empowering Frontline Staff for Client-Centric Empowerment: Frontline staff members, including receptionists and customer service representatives, play a pivotal role in shaping customer relations. Empowering these employees to take ownership of client interactions, resolve issues autonomously, and act as brand ambassadors can significantly enhance the overall client experience. By entrusting frontline staff with the autonomy to address client needs and concerns, salons can foster a client-centric culture that prioritizes personalized care and attention.

Ethical Business Practices and Transparency: Upholding ethical business practices and transparent communication with clients are critical pillars of building strong customer relations. By maintaining transparency in pricing, service details, and product information, salons can build trust and credibility with their client base. Moreover, ethical conduct, such as prioritizing client well-being over sales targets and providing honest recommendations, helps fortify the integrity of customer relations within the salon industry.

Continuous Feedback Integration for Service Enhancement: Integrating client feedback into continuous service enhancement initiatives is essential for nurturing strong customer relations. Actively seeking and incorporating client suggestions, preferences, and critiques into operational improvements demonstrates a dedication to meeting client needs and expectations. By approaching feedback as a catalyst for positive change, salons can build a reputation for attentiveness and responsiveness, elevating the overall client experience.

Proactive Client Engagement Through Personalized Surveys: Proactively engaging clients through personalized surveys can yield valuable insights into their experiences and preferences. Tailoring survey questions to capture specific aspects of the client journey, such as service quality, staff interactions, and facility ambiance, can provide actionable data for refining the salon's customer relations strategies. Additionally, soliciting input from clients signals a commitment to continuous improvement and client-centric service delivery.

Curating Client-Centric Events and Workshops: Hosting client-centric events and workshops can further enhance customer relations by creating opportunities for meaningful engagement and education. From nail care workshops to themed beauty events, salons can facilitate spaces for clients to connect, learn, and engage with the brand on a deeper level. These initiatives not only foster a sense of community but also position the salon as a valuable resource for clients beyond the traditional service offering.

Embracing Client-Centric Innovation and Adaptation: Embracing a client-centric innovation mindset and adaptability can open avenues for building robust customer relations. By actively seeking ways to enhance the client experience, such as introducing new services, incorporating client feedback into product offerings, or embracing technological advancements, salons can demonstrate a commitment to evolving in alignment with client needs and preferences. This forward-thinking approach not only fosters loyalty but also positions the salon as a trusted partner in the client's beauty journey.

Multi-Sensory Client Experience Design: Considering the multi-sensory aspects of the client experience can significantly impact customer relations. From incorporating soothing scents and calming music to providing visually appealing decor, salons can create a holistic sensory experience that resonates with clients on an emotional level. By stimulating multiple senses, salons can evoke positive emotions, relaxation, and a memorable experience that fosters strong customer relations.

Cultivating a Culture of Client-Centric Empathy and Understanding: Instilling a culture of empathy and understanding among salon staff can profoundly influence customer relations. By encouraging staff to cultivate empathy, actively listen to clients' needs, and understand their perspectives, salons can create an environment where clients feel genuinely heard and valued. This client-centric approach to communication and service delivery fosters trust, loyalty, and long-term client satisfaction.

Harnessing Sustainable and Eco-Friendly Practices: In an era where sustainability and eco-consciousness are increasingly valued by consumers, adopting sustainable practices can contribute to building strong customer relations. From using eco-friendlyproducts and packaging to embracing energy-efficient practices, salons can demonstrate a commitment to environmental responsibility that resonates with eco-conscious clients. By aligning with clients' values and contributing to environmental conservation efforts, salons can forge deeper connections with socially and environmentally aware clientele, enhancing customer relations.

Collaborative Client-Input Initiatives: Involving clients in collaborative input initiatives, such as product development consultations or service co-creation workshops, can empower clients and strengthen customer relations. By seeking input and involving clients in decision-making processes, salons demonstrate a commitment to co-creating value with their client base. This collaborative approach fosters a sense of ownership and loyalty among clients, who appreciate the opportunity to actively shape the salon's offerings.

Fostering an Inclusive and Diverse Client Community: Creating an inclusive and diverse client community fosters a sense of belonging and strengthens customer relations. By celebrating diversity, embracing inclusivity, and catering to clients of varied backgrounds and preferences, salons can position themselves as welcoming spaces for all. This inclusive approach not only expands the salon's client base but also cultivates an environment where clients feel understood, respected, and valued.

Benchmarking Service Excellence and Best Practices: Benchmarking service excellence against industry standards and best practices is crucial for building strong customer relations. By continuously measuring and refining service quality, staff performance, and client satisfaction metrics, salons can uphold high standards that resonate with discerning clientele. Striving for service excellence and continuous improvement signals a commitment to delivering exceptional experiences, nurturing positive customer relations.

Customized Client-Care Plans and Recommendations: Offering customized client-care plans and personalized recommendations based on individual needs can strengthen customer relations. By taking a proactive approach to understanding each client's preferences, lifestyle, and nail care goals, salons can tailor their services and recommendations accordingly. This personalized care approach demonstrates attentiveness and fosters a deeper connection, promoting continued loyalty and client satisfaction.

Relationship-Based Customer Retention Strategies: Building customer relations calls for relationship-based customer retention strategies that go beyond transactional interactions. From scheduling follow-up calls to check on client satisfaction to offering exclusive loyalty rewards based on relationship longevity, salons can nurture enduring client connections. By prioritizing ongoing relationship-building efforts, salons can inspire loyalty, advocacy, and long-term retention among their client base.

Nurturing Client-Centric Brand Advocacy: Empowering satisfied clients to become brand advocates can significantly impact customer relations. By fostering a client-centric advocacy program that invites clients to share their experiences, refer new clients, or engage in user-generated content creation, salons can amplify their reach and credibility. The authentic endorsements and recommendations from loyal clients serve as powerful testimonials, further enhancing customer relations and contributing to positive brand perception.

Reflecting Client Diversity in Marketing and Representation: Reflecting client diversity in marketing campaigns and brand representation is vital for building strong customer relations. By showcasing diverse clientele in promotional materials, social media content, and advertising, salons signal inclusivity and relatability. This representation not only resonates with clients from varied backgrounds but also fosters a sense of connection and belonging, strengthening customer relations on a broader scale.

Quickreads Presents:: Open Your Own Nail Salon

Expanding Your Nail Salon Business

Market Analysis:
Before expanding your nail salon business, it is crucial to conduct a thorough market analysis to identify potential growth opportunities and customer demographics. This analysis should include researching the local market, competition, and industry trends to determine the viability of expansion. Understanding the demographic makeup of the area surrounding your salon is important. Factors such as age, occupation, income level, and lifestyle preferences will influence the types of services and products that will be in demand. Additionally, analyzing the spending patterns and beauty preferences of potential customers will provide valuable insights into tailoring the salon's offerings to meet their needs.

When conducting market analysis, it's essential to gather comprehensive data about the local community to understand the target market's behavior and preferences. This can involve researching census data, consumer spending patterns, and local economic trends to gain insights into the purchasing power and lifestyle choices of the community. Social and cultural factors should also be considered, as they can significantly impact beauty and wellness preferences. By identifying these factors, the salon can tailor its marketing and service offerings to align with the specific needs and desires of the local community.

Furthermore, studying the competitive landscape will help identify any niche areas that are underserved or untapped, providing an opportunity for the salon to differentiate itself and attract a loyal customer base. This may involve assessing the strengths and weaknesses of existing competitors, understanding their pricing strategies, service quality, and customer satisfaction levels. Identifying potential gaps in the market and areas where the salon can excel can inform the development of a unique value proposition that sets it apart from competitors.

An important aspect of market analysis is also understanding industry trends and developments. This includes staying abreast of new nail care techniques, product innovations, and evolving customer preferences. This insight can inform the salon's expansion strategy, such as introducing new services or incorporating trendy nail art techniques that resonate with the target market.

Financial Considerations:

Expanding a nail salon business requires significant financial investment. It is essential to develop a comprehensive financial plan that outlines the costs associated with expansion, such as new equipment, additional staff, marketing expenses, and facility upgrades. Securing funding through loans, investors, or other avenues may be necessary to support the expansion. It is important to evaluate the best financing options available, weighing the benefits and risks of each.

Building a strong financial foundation for expansion is crucial for long-term success and stability. Conducting a cost-benefit analysis to assess the potential return on investment and the timeline for recouping the initial outlay is essential. Moreover, creating realistic revenue projections and cash flow forecasts can help in understanding the financial implications of expansion and ensure that the business is adequately capitalized to support growth.

To effectively manage the financial aspects of expansion, it is imperative to work closely with accountants, financial advisors, and lenders to ensure that the financial plan aligns with the salon's growth objectives. Moreover, exploring potential tax incentives, grants, or other financial assistance programs for small businesses can help alleviate some of the financial burden of expansion.

Furthermore, it's crucial to consider the potential impacts of economic fluctuations and market uncertainties on the expansion plans. Conducting scenario analyses and stress-testing financial models can help mitigate risks and ensure the financial resilience of the salon during periods of economic volatility.

Operational Strategies:
Expanding a nail salon business involves operational changes to accommodate increased demand and clientele. This may include hiring and training additional staff, optimizing scheduling and appointment management, and implementing operational efficiencies to handle higher volume. Effectively managing the supply chain to ensure seamless procurement of inventory and products is vital for meeting the demands of an expanded customer base. Additionally, expanding the range of services offered and diversifying product offerings can enhance the salon's appeal to a broader customer base.

It is essential to carefully assess the current operational workflow and identify areas that need to be streamlined or enhanced to ensure a seamless transition into the expansion phase. This may involve revisiting standard operating procedures, workflow optimization, and implementing technology solutions to improve operational efficiency. Automation of administrative tasks, such as inventory management, payroll processing, and customer communications, can free up time for staff to focus on delivering exceptional service to clients.

Moreover, the introduction of new services or product lines as part of the expansion strategy necessitates thorough operational planning. This includes considering the training needs of existing and new staff, creating standardized procedures to maintain consistency in service quality, and ensuring that the physical space can accommodate the expanded offerings without compromising the customer experience.

Additionally, developing strategies to monitor and maintain service quality while scaling the business is paramount. This may involve implementing customer feedback systems, performance metrics, and regular training programs to uphold the salon's reputation for excellence as it grows. By proactively addressing operational challenges and optimizing workflows, the salon can position itself for sustainable expansion and operational success.

Customer Relationship Management:
As the business expands, maintaining strong customer relationships becomes even more critical. Implementing customer loyalty programs, personalized communication strategies, and gathering customer feedback can help retain existing clients and attract new ones. Building a robust customer relationship management system is essential for sustaining growth and promoting positive word-of-mouth marketing.

Developing a deep understanding of customer preferences and behavior through data analysis and market research can guide the development of personalized marketing strategies, tailored promotions, and service offerings that resonate with the target audience. Leveraging customer relationship management (CRM) platforms and data analytics tools can provide valuable insights into customer lifecycle management, allowing the salon to create targeted marketing campaigns and personalized experiences for each customer.

Moreover, embracing technology to enhance customer experience, such as online booking systems, personalized email marketing, and social media engagement, can further strengthen the bond with customers and create a sense of community around the salon. By leveraging digital channels and social platforms, the salon can foster ongoing engagement with customers, share educational content, and solicit feedback to continuously improve the customer experience.

Consistently seeking feedback and implementing improvements based on customer suggestions can foster a strong sense of loyalty and advocacy, driving long-term success for the expanded nail salon business. Building a customer-centric culture within the salon, where staff are trained to prioritize personalized service and exceed customer expectations, can further solidify the salon's reputation as a trusted partner in beauty and wellness. By prioritizing customer relationships and creating a seamless, enjoyable experience, the salon can position itself for sustainable growth and long-term success in the competitive beauty industry.

Quickreads Presents:: Open Your Own Nail Salon

Embracing Innovation

In any industry, embracing innovation is pivotal for long-term success and growth, and the nail salon business is no exception. This chapter will dive into the multifaceted aspects of innovation, exploring how technological advancements, trend awareness, and sustainable practices can propel your nail salon to new heights of success.

Technological innovation is a cornerstone of modern nail salon operations, offering opportunities to enhance customer experience, streamline processes, and increase efficiency. As technological advancements continue to revolutionize the beauty industry, nail salons can leverage cutting-edge tools and software to stay competitive. For instance, the deployment of advanced nail art printers and digital design software can provide a myriad of creative options for customers, while automated scheduling and appointment management systems can streamline operations and improve customer service.

Moreover, the adoption of customer relationship management (CRM) systems can offer valuable insights into customer preferences, leading to more personalized marketing efforts and targeted promotions. Embracing technology also extends to digital marketing strategies, such as social media management, online booking, and e-commerce capabilities – all of which can expand your customer base and boost sales.

Additionally, incorporating virtual reality (VR) and augmented reality (AR) experiences into your nail salon can provide customers with an immersive and interactive way to preview different nail designs and color options, enhancing their overall salon experience. By allowing clients to virtually try on various nail styles and colors before the actual application, you can increase customer satisfaction and confidence in their choices, ultimately leading to higher sales and repeat business.

In conjunction with technological advancements, staying abreast of emerging trends in nail art, techniques, and products remains pivotal for sustained success. Nail salons can achieve this by fostering a culture of creativity and curiosity among their team members and encouraging them to attend industry events, workshops, and conferences to keep up with the latest developments in nail care and design.

To further enhance trend awareness, collaborating with fashion influencers, partnering with beauty content creators, and participating in fashion shows or editorial photoshoots can help your salon stay at the forefront of the latest trends in nail art and design. By aligning your offerings with the broader trends in fashion and lifestyle, your salon can attract a more fashion-forward clientele, setting itself apart from competitors and solidifying its position as a trendsetting destination.

Moreover, the integration of sustainable practices into nail salon operations has become increasingly crucial in response to growing environmental concerns. As consumers become more conscious of the impact of their purchasing decisions, offering eco-friendly and non-toxic nail care options has garnered heightened interest. Exploring partnerships with environmentally responsible nail polish brands and adopting sustainable manufacturing practices can demonstrate your salon's commitment to eco-consciousness, appealing to environmentally aware clients and setting your business apart as a sustainable leader in the industry.

Furthermore, prioritizing energy-efficient lighting and equipment, utilizing water-saving technologies, and implementing recycling programs can reduce the environmental footprint of your salon while resonating with eco-conscious customers. Creating an inviting and sustainable salon environment can also act as a marketing differentiator, attracting clientele who prioritize ethical and sustainable practices when choosing beauty and wellness services.

In conclusion, embracing innovation in the nail salon business encompasses leveraging technological advancements, staying ahead of emerging trends, and integrating sustainable practices. By proactively incorporating innovative solutions into your operations, you can elevate the customer experience, drive business growth, and establish your salon as a forward-thinking leader in the ever-evolving world of beauty and wellness services.

Quickreads Presents:: Open Your Own Nail Salon

<S: Achieving Work-Life Balance

In the fast-paced and demanding environment of the nail salon industry, achieving work-life balance can be a significant challenge. With long hours spent attending to clients, managing staff, and handling administrative tasks, salon owners and technicians often find themselves struggling to maintain a sense of equilibrium between their professional and personal lives. This chapter will delve into strategies and techniques for attaining a healthy work-life balance in the nail salon industry.

Time Management: Implementing effective time management strategies is crucial for achieving work-life balance. Utilizing scheduling software, setting specific working hours, and adhering to a structured routine can help salon owners and technicians allocate time for work and personal activities. Time blocking techniques, where specific time slots are allocated for different tasks, can help in prioritizing and safeguarding personal time, allowing for a better work-life balance.

Delegating Responsibilities: Delegation allows salon owners to distribute tasks among their staff, reducing their workload and providing them with the flexibility to focus on personal engagements. Assigning responsibilities to capable team members fosters a sense of ownership and empowerment while creating a more balanced work environment. Furthermore, conducting regular training and skill development sessions for staff ensures that they are equipped to handle delegated tasks effectively, reducing the owner's need for constant oversight.

Setting Boundaries: Establishing clear boundaries between work and personal life is essential. This may involve designating specific days off, refraining from checking work-related emails during personal time, and creating a conducive environment for relaxation and rejuvenation outside of the salon. Additionally, developing a habit of mindfulness and setting aside time for hobbies or activities that promote personal fulfillment can further reinforce these boundaries, contributing to a healthier work-life balance.

Embracing Technology: Leveraging technology can streamline salon operations, freeing up time for salon owners and technicians. Online booking systems, digital marketing platforms, and automated administrative tools can minimize manual tasks and allow for more efficient time management. Moreover, utilizing customer relationship management (CRM) tools and analytics can provide insights into customer preferences and behavior, enabling more targeted and effective marketing efforts, ultimately reducing the time and effort required for client acquisition and retention.

Self-Care Practices: Prioritizing self-care is vital for maintaining a healthy work-life balance. Encouraging staff to take breaks, offering wellness programs, and promoting mindfulness and relaxation techniques within the salon environment can contribute to overall well-being. Additionally, incorporating physical amenities such as comfortable staff break areas, ergonomic workstations, and relaxation spaces within the salon can be conducive to staff well-being, reducing stress and enhancing work-life balance.

Communication and Collaboration: Open and transparent communication between salon owners, staff, and clients is essential for creating a supportive work culture. Encouraging teamwork, providing avenues for feedback, and fostering a collaborative atmosphere can alleviate stress and promote work-life harmony. Implementing regular team meetings and feedback sessions, where all stakeholders have a platform to express their thoughts and concerns, can strengthen the salon's community and enhance work satisfaction, ultimately contributing to a better work-life balance.

Flexibility and Adaptability: Recognizing the dynamic nature of the industry, salon owners should embrace flexibility and adaptability in their approach to work-life balance. Being open to adjusting schedules, accommodating staff needs, and embracing change can enhance overall harmony within the salon. Additionally, creating a culture of flexibility and adaptability within the salon environment, where innovative ideas and new approaches are encouraged, can foster a sense of excitement and fulfillment among staff, thereby contributing to a more balanced and rewarding work-life experience.

By implementing these strategies, salon owners and technicians can achieve a more sustainable work-life balance, leading to improved well-being, enhanced productivity, and a more rewarding professional experience.

Quickreads Presents:: Open Your Own Nail Salon

<S:Fulfilling Your Entrepreneurial Dreams

Environmental Sustainability and Green Practices
  - Embracing environmentally sustainable practices within your nail salon business can demonstrate a commitment to reducing environmental impact and aligning with eco-conscious consumer preferences. This can involve implementing measures to minimize waste through recycling programs, energy-efficient technologies, and eco-friendly product lines. Additionally, consider incorporating sustainable design and decor elements into your salon to create an eco-chic ambiance that resonates with environmentally conscious clientele. Explore opportunities to source sustainable and ethically produced nail care products, such as non-toxic polishes and eco-friendly nail treatments, to further solidify your salon's green initiatives.

Community Engagement and Social Responsibility
  - Engaging with the local community and supporting social causes can enhance your nail salon's reputation and contribute to meaningful social impact. Consider participating in local events, collaborating with charitable organizations, or initiating community outreach programs to foster goodwill and establish your salon as a socially responsible entity. Demonstrating a genuine interest in community well-being can cultivate customer loyalty and a positive brand image, while also fostering a sense of pride among your employees as they contribute to meaningful initiatives within the community.

Data Analytics and Performance Metrics
  - Leveraging data analytics and performance metrics can provide valuable insights into client preferences, sales trends, and operational efficiency. Implementing data-driven decision-making processes enables you to identify opportunities for business growth, optimize marketing strategies, and enhance the overall client experience. Utilize key performance indicators (KPIs) to monitor business performance and make informed strategic decisions. By analyzing client retention rates, average spend per visit, and seasonal trends, you can tailor your offerings and marketing efforts to better meet the evolving needs of your clientele, ultimately driving sustainable business growth.

Industry Associations and Networking
  - Building connections within the beauty and wellness industry through participation in

industry associations, networking events, and trade shows can offer valuable opportunities for learning, collaboration, and business expansion. Engage with fellow professionals, stay abreast of industry trends, and seek mentorship from experienced peers to gain insights and guidance for advancing your nail salon business. Collaborating with industry peers can also open doors to partnerships, joint marketing initiatives, and access to specialized training and resources, further propelling your salon's success within the industry.

Intellectual Property Protection
 - Safeguarding your brand identity, creative works, and innovative business concepts through intellectual property protection is essential for preserving the unique assets of your nail salon business. Consider trademarks for your salon name, logo, and proprietary nail art designs, as well as legal protections for any original content or innovations, to prevent unauthorized use and establish legal recourse against infringement. Additionally, you may explore the process of patenting unique salon equipment or processes, further solidifying your position as an innovator and leader in the industry.

Marketing Personalization and Client Segmentation
 - Implement personalized marketing strategies by segmenting your client base and tailoring promotional efforts to specific demographics, preferences, and purchasing behaviors. Utilize customer relationship management (CRM) systems to gather insights and create targeted marketing campaigns, such as personalized offers, loyalty rewards, and special event invitations, to captivate and retain diverse client segments. By understanding the nuances of different customer segments, you can craft compelling marketing messages, refine service offerings, and elevate the overall experience for each client group, fostering deeper loyalty and satisfaction.

Digital Branding and Online Presence
 - Building a strong digital brand presence is paramount in reaching and engaging with modern consumers. Establish a polished and cohesive brand identity across your website, social media platforms, and online marketing channels to create a compelling and consistent brand experience. Utilize captivating visual content, engaging storytelling, and responsive communication to foster a strong digital connection with your audience. Additionally, consider innovative digital experiences such as virtual nail art consultations, online booking features, and interactive social media campaigns, creating an immersive and interactive journey for your clients that extends beyond the physical salon experience.

Legal Compliance and Risk Management
 - Prioritizing legal compliance and risk management through thorough understanding and adherence to business laws, contractual obligations, and liability protection measures is crucial for the long-term sustainability of your nail salon business. Consult legal professionals to ensure full compliance with industry regulations, protect against potential legal disputes, and fortify your enterprise against unforeseen liabilities. Additionally,

developing robust risk management protocols to address safety, security, and financial contingencies will safeguard your business from potential disruptions and legal challenges, offering peace of mind as you grow and expand your salon.

Retail and Product Diversification
- Enhance the revenue potential of your nail salon business by expanding into retail offerings and diversifying your product line. Consider curating a selection of high-quality nail care products, salon-exclusive merchandise, and beauty accessories to supplement your service offerings and provide clients with premium at-home care solutions, enhancing their overall beauty experience. By understanding the needs and preferences of your clientele, you can introduce and showcase curated product lines, collaborate with reputable beauty brands, and create a comprehensive retail experience that extends the benefits of your salon services beyond the salon walls.

Crisis Communication and Reputation Management
- Prepare a comprehensive crisis communication plan to effectively manage potential public relations challenges and protect the reputation of your nail salon. Establish clear communication protocols, spokesperson roles, and strategies for addressing crises transparently and responsibly, ensuring prompt resolution and damage control in the event of unforeseen reputation-threatening situations. Conducting regular reputation audits and scenario planning can help your salon anticipate and effectively navigate potential issues, maintain trust with clients, and demonstrate resilience as a reputable and trustworthy business entity.

Cultural Competency and Diversity Training
- Foster a culturally competent and inclusive workplace by providing diversity training to your staff and establishing a welcoming environment that celebrates cultural diversity. Encourage open dialogue, respect for differing perspectives, and sensitivity to diverse backgrounds, nurturing a workplace culture that embraces inclusivity and promotes mutual understanding among team members and clients alike. By fostering an inclusive and diverse salon environment, you can cultivate a sense of belonging among your staff, attract a wider and more diverse clientele, and contribute positively to social and cultural diversity within the local community.

Technology Integration and Automation
- Embracing technology integration and automation in your nail salon business can streamline operations and enhance the client experience. Consider implementing appointment scheduling software, inventory management systems, and point-of-sale solutions to optimize efficiency. Furthermore, explore digital tools for client communication, feedback management, and online booking services to elevate convenience and accessibility for your clientele. By leveraging technology and automation, you can improve operational efficiency, optimize staff productivity, and create a seamless and modern client

experience that reflects your commitment to innovation and convenience.

Health and Safety Standards
- Upholding stringent health and safety standards is paramount in the nail salon industry to ensure client well-being and maintain regulatory compliance. Train your staff in proper sanitation and hygiene practices, adhere to industry-specific health regulations, and prioritize the use of high-quality, non-toxic products to safeguard both your clients and employees. Regularly review and update safety protocols to align with industry best practices. Additionally, staying informed about emerging safety standards, such as ventilation requirements, chemical exposure limits, and infection control best practices, will empower your salon to remain at the forefront of industry safety and client care.

Supply Chain Management and Vendor Relations
- Establishing strong relationships with reputable suppliersCertainly, here are the rest of the points:

Supply Chain Management and Vendor Relations (continued)
- Establishing strong relationships with reputable suppliers is essential for efficient supply chain management in your nail salon business. Seek suppliers who offer high-quality products, reliable delivery, and competitive pricing to ensure consistency and reliability in your inventory. Cultivate transparent and communicative relationships with your vendors, fostering collaboration and mutual support to address evolving business needs and maintain a robust supply chain that meets the demands of your salon's operation.

Innovation and Adaptability
- Embrace a culture of innovation and adaptability by encouraging creative thinking, experimentation, and open-mindedness within your salon. Foster a dynamic work environment that values continuous learning, forward thinking, and adaptability to change, empowering your team to embrace new trends, technologies, and business strategies. By staying receptive to innovation and adaptability, your salon can evolve to meet the shifting demands of the beauty industry, positioning your business as a cutting-edge leader that is ready to capitalize on emerging opportunities and challenges.

Mental Health and Wellness Support
- Prioritize the mental health and wellness of your employees by providing access to resources, support programs, and a healthy workplace culture that promotes holistic well-being. Address stress management, burnout prevention, and work-life balance by offering mental health awareness training, access to counseling services, and wellness initiatives that nurture a positive and supportive work environment. By investing in the mental and emotional wellness of your team, you can cultivate a resilient and engaged staff, ultimately enhancing client satisfaction and sustaining a thriving salon environment.

Corporate Social Responsibility Initiatives
   - Engage in corporate social responsibility initiatives to drive positive social impact and community outreach. Consider supporting charitable causes, environmental conservation programs, or local community development projects to showcase your salon's commitment to social responsibility. By aligning your business with meaningful social causes and spearheading initiatives that contribute to the greater good, your nail salon can inspire client loyalty, promote community goodwill, and solidify its reputation as a conscientious and socially responsible business entity.

Business Expansion and Franchising Opportunities
   - Explore the potential for business expansion, franchise opportunities, or strategic partnerships to grow and scale your nail salon business. Investigate the viability of franchising your salon brand, opening new locations, or forming alliances with complementary beauty and wellness businesses to expand your market presence. Adhere to diligent planning, market research, and franchise development protocols to ensure seamless business expansion and maximize growth potential while maintaining the integrity and unique identity of your salon brand.

Professional Development and Industry Training
   - Invest in continuous professional development and industry-specific training for your nail salon staff to refine their skills, stay updated on industry trends, and foster a culture of excellence within your salon. Offer ongoing education, specialized workshops, and certification programs to enhance the expertise of your team, enabling them to deliver exceptional service, master new techniques, and stay ahead of industry innovations. By prioritizing professional development, your salon can cultivate a team of highly skilled professionals and elevate the quality of service offered to discerning clients.

Succession Planning and Long-Term Vision
   - Develop a comprehensive succession plan and long-term vision for your nail salon business to safeguard its continuity and legacy. Identify potential leaders within your organization, establish clear protocols for leadership transitions, and outline a strategic succession roadmap to ensure seamless continuity in the event of leadership changes. Additionally, define a long-term vision that encapsulates the future growth, diversification, and legacy of your salon, guiding your business toward sustainable success and enduring relevance within the beauty and wellness industry.

Crisis Resilience and Business Continuity
   - Prepare your nail salon business for unforeseen challenges and crises by implementing robust crisis resilience and business continuity strategies. Assess potential vulnerabilities, establish contingency plans, and fortify your business against disruptions through effective risk mitigation, disaster recovery protocols, and financial resilience measures. By anticipating and proactively addressing potential crises, your salon can maintain seamless

operations, protect its brand reputation, and ensure the long-term viability of the business even in the face of unexpected adversities.

Client Experience Enhancement and Feedback Integration
- Continuously enhance the client experience and integrate client feedback into your salon's operational and service improvement efforts. Utilize client satisfaction surveys, feedback mechanisms, and focus groups to gather insights and identify areas for refinement and innovation. By prioritizing client feedback and actively implementing improvement initiatives, your salon can deliver personalized, high-quality experiences that resonate with clients, cultivate brand loyalty, and position your salon as a destination of choice for discerning consumers seeking unparalleled beauty and wellness experiences.

These comprehensive strategies can serve as a roadmap for entrepreneurs seeking to thrive and lead in the competitive nail salon industry, driving business success while prioritizing clients, employees, and the broader community.

Quickreads Presents:: Open Your Own Nail Salon

<S: Overcoming Entrepreneurial Challenges

Financial Management:
Effective financial management is a cornerstone of success for entrepreneurs in the nail salon industry. Beyond monitoring daily expenses, it is crucial to establish a comprehensive financial plan that spans both short-term and long-term objectives. A detailed financial plan should account for various scenarios, including different revenue growth strategies, cost-cutting measures, and the establishment of emergency funds to mitigate the impact of unforeseen financial challenges. It is imperative for nail salon business owners to diligently track their cash flow, as well as monitor and analyze key financial metrics to ensure the business remains financially healthy and sustainable.

To achieve this, implementing a robust accounting system is essential. Using accounting software can streamline financial record-keeping and facilitate easy access to real-time financial data, enabling informed decision-making. Moreover, establishing a system for regular financial reporting and budget monitoring can provide valuable insights into the financial health of the business, allowing for timely adjustments to optimize cash flow and profitability.

In addition, the utilization of key performance indicators (KPIs) is vital for assessing the financial performance of the nail salon. KPIs such as average revenue per customer, customer retention rates, and inventory turnover can offer actionable insights into the efficiency of the business operations and customer satisfaction levels. These metrics empower the management to make data-driven decisions and identify areas for improvement in the financial management of the salon.

Regulatory Compliance:
The nail salon industry operates within a complex regulatory landscape, necessitating a meticulous approach to ensure full compliance with local, state, and federal laws. Entrepreneurs must navigate a range of regulatory requirements, including obtaining the necessary business licenses, adhering to health and safety standards, and complying with labor regulations such as minimum wage and overtime requirements.

Ensuring compliance with environmental regulations is also crucial. This includes proper disposal of chemical waste and adherence to air quality standards to minimize the environmental impact of salon operations. It is essential for salon owners to stay informed about changing regulations, such as updates to chemical safety standards for nail products and evolving environmental sustainability initiatives, to avoid legal repercussions and maintain a positive public image. Deliberate efforts should be made to periodically review and update compliance protocols to align with the latest regulatory developments, thereby safeguarding the business from potential fines or legal issues.

Moreover, fostering strong relationships with legal and compliance experts can provide valuable guidance and support in navigating the intricacies of regulatory requirements. Seeking legal counsel when necessary and conducting regular internal audits to assess compliance can help mitigate legal risks and uphold the reputation of the nail salon business.

Staffing and Training:
The recruitment and retention of skilled staff are pivotal to the success of a nail salon business. In addition to offering competitive salaries and benefits, entrepreneurs should invest in continuous training programs to enhance the skills and expertise of their team. This investment not only ensures high-quality service delivery but also demonstrates a commitment to professional development, fostering a positive work culture and improving employee morale.

Training programs should encompass a wide range of skills, catering to the diverse needs of clients and staying updated on industry trends. This may include nail art techniques, customer service, product knowledge, and health and safety protocols. By equipping employees with these skills, a salon can differentiate itself through exceptional service and meet the evolving demands of discerning customers.

Implementing mentorship programs that pair experienced staff with new hires can contribute to knowledge transfer and skill development within the salon. Moreover, creating an inclusive, supportive work environment is crucial for staff to thrive and flourish in their roles. Providing clear career development pathways and opportunities for growth within the company can enhance employee satisfaction and loyalty.

Marketing and Differentiation:
In a competitive market, strategic marketing efforts are essential for attracting and retaining customers in the nail salon industry. Understanding the target demographic and tailoring marketing campaigns accordingly is fundamental. Leveraging social media platforms and developing engaging, informative content can expand the reach of the nail salon business and foster a community of loyal customers.

In addition to digital marketing, implementing localized marketing strategies, such as community events and partnerships, can increase brand visibility and attract new clientele. Differentiating the salon by offering unique services, eco-friendly products, or specialized nail care treatments can create a distinct brand identity that resonates with clients, setting the business apart from competitors in a crowded market.

Gathering and analyzing customer feedback and market research can inform marketing strategies, ensuring that the salon offers services and experiences that cater to the evolving preferences and needs of its clientele. Tailoring promotions and loyalty programs based on customer behavior and preferences can foster long-term relationships and drive customer retention.

Risk Management:
Mitigating risks across various dimensions is essential for the resilience of a nail salon business. Understanding potential workplace hazards and implementing robust safety protocols to protect both employees and clients is paramount. This requires ongoing assessments of the salon's physical environment to identify and address potential safety risks. Additionally, staying informed about industry best practices in salon safety and hygiene is crucial to upholding a safe and secure environment for all stakeholders.

In terms of insurance coverage, it is essential for nail salon owners to work with knowledgeable insurance professionals to secure appropriate coverage. This may include general liability insurance to protect against third-party claims, worker's compensation insurance to provide coverage for workplace injuries, and professional indemnity insurance to safeguard against claims of professional negligence. Developing a thorough understanding of the scope and limitations of insurance coverage is critical to mitigating potential liabilities and protecting the financial well-being of the business.

Moreover, implementing data security measures, particularly in managing client information and payment transactions, is essential to protect against cyber threats and privacy breaches. This may include utilizing secure payment processing systems, encrypting sensitive data, and establishing clear protocols for data access and protection. By fostering a culture of risk awareness and proactively addressing potential vulnerabilities, entrepreneurs can fortify the foundation of their nail salon business and build resilience in an ever-changing business landscape. Additionally, conducting regular risk assessments and creating contingency plans for various scenarios, such as natural disasters or economic downturns, can help the business adapt and thrive in challenging circumstances.

Quickreads Presents:: Open Your Own Nail Salon

<S:Embracing Change

Leveraging Technology for Enhanced Customer Experience

Embracing change within the nail salon business involves leveraging technology to enhance the customer experience and streamline operations. By adopting salon management software, nail salons can facilitate online booking, appointment reminders, and client communication, making the booking process more convenient for customers. Additionally, implementing digital payment systems not only improves transaction efficiency but also reduces physical contact, addressing concerns related to hygiene and safety. Furthermore, embracing digital marketing strategies, such as social media engagement and personalized email campaigns, can help nail salons connect with their audience, build brand awareness, and foster customer loyalty in a competitive market.

Cultivating Sustainable Practices and Environmental Responsibility

Embracing change in the nail salon business also encompasses cultivating sustainable practices and prioritizing environmental responsibility. Salon owners can opt for eco-friendly and cruelty-free nail care products, minimizing their ecological footprint while aligning with the growing demand for sustainable beauty options. Additionally, implementing green initiatives, such as energy-efficient lighting, recycling programs, and reducing water consumption, can contribute to a more environmentally conscious operation. By embracing sustainability, nail salons can appeal to eco-conscious consumers and position themselves as advocates for responsible environmental stewardship within the beauty industry.

Emphasizing Staff Well-Being and Professional Development

Embracing change in the nail salon business involves prioritizing staff well-being and fostering opportunities for professional development. Salon owners can create a supportive and nurturing work environment by providing resources for mental health and offering work-life balance initiatives. Furthermore, investing in training and mentorship programs can empower team members to grow their skills, advance their careers, and feel valued within the salon community. By emphasizing staff well-being and professional development, nail salons can cultivate a motivated and skilled workforce, which directly contributes to the delivery of exceptional customer experiences and long-term business success.

Managing Customer Data for Personalized Services

Embracing change also entails leveraging customer data to deliver personalized services and tailor experiences to individual preferences. Implementing customer relationship management (CRM) systems allows nail salons to capture and analyze client information, such as service history, product preferences, and special occasions, enabling personalized recommendations and targeted promotional offers. By utilizing data-driven insights, salons can build stronger customer relationships, anticipate needs, and exceed expectations, ultimately fostering customer satisfaction and loyalty.

Embracing Diversity and Cultural Competence

Beyond inclusivity, embracing change in the nail salon business involves recognizing and celebrating diversity in its broadest sense. This includes embracing cultural competence by understanding and respecting the cultural backgrounds and traditions of diverse clientele. Salon owners can encourage cultural awareness training for staff to ensure that the salon environment is inclusive and welcoming to customers of varying ethnicities, backgrounds, and customs. By embracing diversity and cultural competence, nail salons can create an environment where all clients feel valued, respected, and understood, thereby fostering a sense of belonging and trust within the salon.

Evolving Business Models for Flexibility and Innovation

Embracing change also necessitates evolving traditional business models to embrace flexibility and innovation. Nail salons can explore hybrid models, incorporating mobile services, pop-up events, or partnerships with complementary businesses to reach a broader audience and adapt to evolving consumer preferences. Furthermore, embracing innovation may involve introducing new service offerings, such as nail art masterclasses, DIY kits, or subscription-based models, to diversify revenue streams and stay ahead of industry trends. By evolving business models, nail salons can demonstrate agility, creativity, and resilience in the face of change, ensuring long-term success in a dynamic market.

By delving into these multifaceted dimensions of embracing change within the nail salon business, owners can proactively adapt to industry developments, consumer needs, and societal shifts, positioning their salons for sustained relevance and prosperity in a rapidly evolving landscape.

www.ingramcontent.com/pod-product-compliance
Lightning Source LLC
Chambersburg PA
CBHW050112230526
45470CB00004B/1801